GW00730195

What's a Nice Jewish Boy Like You Doing in the First Baptist Church?

by Bob Friedman

Trinity Publications

Second Printing, 1973
Third Printing, 1973
Fourth Printing, 1976
Fifth Printing, 1976

1980's Edition
Published 1982 by
Trinity Press

Library of Congress Catalog Card No. 72-75591
ISBN 0-8307-0161-3

Scripture quoted from
New American Standard Bible. © The Lockman
Foundation, 1971. Used by permission.

Preface to 1980's Edition

What's a Nice Jewish Boy Like You Doing in the First Baptist Church? was written over ten years ago when young men were "dudes" or "cats" and the dudes were often "heads" as were their "chicks" or "dolls."

Keep this in mind as you read about "bad vibes" putting some dude on a "bummer," when just hours before he was really groovin' after a night at a crash pad.

Also, something can't be good, it must be *cool*, etc., etc., etc. Yet the story of how I met up with Messiah Jesus is as relevant today as it was several years ago.

To keep you posted on certain key figures mentioned:

Arthur and Sherrie Blessitt had just had their daughter Joy when we met. They've since added Joshua, Joseph and Jerusalem who, along with Gina and Joel, make for eight blessed Blessitts.

Six months after we met Arthur picked up a twelve-foot wooden cross and proceeded to walk around the world with it. Several times. And he's still at it . . .

Barry Wood left the Strip for Lubbock, Texas, where, God forbid he would ever need a blood transfusion, it would be guaranteed to come from a Southern Baptist.

Martin Rosen of the ABMJ fell into a giant pot of chicken soup and reappeared as Moishe Rosen, leader of a great group called Jews for Jesus. Jews for Y'shua?

As for me, well . . . the final chapters will bring you up to date on how I stepped into the Spirit . . .

Bob Friedman

Contents

Testimony of a Jewish Blah

If this is your first introduction to the crazy world of the Jewish-Christian I suggest you do two things: first, get it out of your head all priests look like Spencer Tracy; secondly, remember at one point in history your rabbi was only a man.

With these facts rooted firmly in mind it will come as no surprise to you that a Jewish-Christian is a loving soul who eats cream cheese and ham for breakfast and plants a tree in Israel at Eastertime.

Then again, this wouldn't exactly eliminate many temple goers . . . .

But on with my story of how a Bar Mitzvahed, almost-confirmed, college-graduate Jewish Blah discovered the happiest years of my life were *not* spent as president of the temple youth group while in junior high school.

No, I was a typical native-Californian-type dude who stormed out of pre-confirmation class at the age of fourteen because the teacher (snicker!) believed most of the Bible was true.

Then, having bulled my way through high school and college by playing a favorite game of "Don't-Study-And-The-Tests-Will-Be-A-Real-Challenge," I worked as a newspaper reporter for a few years.

A newspaper reporter as a job for a nice Jewish boy? So when can you be publisher? Phooey.

Listen, it was in the summer of 1969 when we had a very slow news day in Los Angeles. The city editor, the burning end of his cigar resting comfortably on his tongue, motioned me toward his desk with a quick wave of an eyebrow.

"Roll up to the Strip with a photog and check out this nut who's chained himself to a cross or somethin'."

"Who's what?"

"Why ain't you back yet?"

It takes a while to understand editors . . .

As we dodged the dollies up on Sunset Boulevard we stumbled across this weird cat from Mississippi standing by a ten-foot-high wooden cross. *Oy.* He's got a chain around his waist which winds up and curls itself around the top of the cross.

It didn't startle me. There are so many heads in Hollywood that anything goes—and everything comes. Anyway, I knew if the United Jewish Welfare Fund could pull a stunt like this they'd raise enough bread to buy Cairo.

2

This dude's name must have been a brainstorm of his PR agency. You ready? Blessitt. Arthur *Blessitt*. An *evangelist*. (It's as if my old rabbi called himself Ben Torah.) I think he supplied his own Southern accent and Bible.

O.K. Why the press conference? I was flanked by a few other reporters.

"Well, this here Bible was a gettin' too close to that there booze!"

Arthur (he liked to be called Arthur) told his story. He had had a Christian coffee house, called His Place, on the Strip right next to these topless, bottomless, lustful centers of man's decadence.

It seems as if the owners of these free-enterprise establishments had put pressure on Arthur's landlord (not to be confused with the other Lord) and they refused to renew his lease.

He vowed to crash on the sidewalk—and not eat —until someone would rent him a building on the Strip. I drew a Star of David at the top of my notepad to remain objective about the whole thing.

I thought his story was absurd, since most of the guys who stagger in and out of those bars are only getting drunk because they feel so guilty about missing church week after week.

"Hey, Arthur," I smirked, "what does the cross do for ya? Give you good posture or something?"

He's cool, right? Arthur just grins as wide as a Dixie sunset and stares me right in the eye.

"Shucks, man, I'm just groovin' on Jesus. He's an eternal trip, a new high!"

Can you believe it? This cat's been eating black-eyed peas and grits for so long that he thinks he's

3

found something heavier than acid or speed. I never did dope, typical of a 25-year-old Jewish Blah that year, but I was familiar with all the ups and downs.

Then Arthur begins talking about God and like that. Now mind you, I had heard of Him before. For example, when the rabbi would promote the B'nai B'rith car wash someone would sneeze and half the congregation would cry out: "God bless you!"

Several ex-heads and society's misfits swarmed around Arthur, parroting everything he said and providing some original copy of their own.

Yet these dudes *did* have something I didn't have. Lights. Built-in lights. In their eyes. Sure, the sun was hitting them, right? My imagination, right? Nope. They had light flowing from within. Weird.

I wrote the copy up and, cynical as he was, the editor gave it a pretty good spread.

That night, with nothing to do, I decided to check up on Arthur. Not so much as a devotion to duty (Blahs don't have that) but simple curiosity as to how Arthur was doing.

It was a real trip just to rap with him. It was obvious I had found one of the nicest, sweetest, misled, *fermished* (dingy) Southerners in the whole cotton-pickin' world.

Unable to tear myself away from my business blood, I kept wondering how I might market that light those disciples of his had. Batteries? Reflectors? Whatever the source, they needed a good Jewish manager.

4

Concentrating on *his* business, Arthur would often ask me to pray with him as I casually dropped by night after night. I didn't have the heart to tell him I was Jewish.

Besides, I could never kneel down on the sidewalk with him and pray. My mother would kill me if I ruined my slacks.

Let's face it. Scientific man will learn enough to save his world. All of the famines, pestilences, riots, crime, drugs and poisoned food can be wiped away like mosquitoes by super technology.

I didn't need anyone else to get me right with God as Arthur insisted. It was enough to help a few old ladies across the street and pay fifty dollars for a seat in temple at Yom Kippur. Then, after I die, the Big Rabbi in the Sky would pat me on the head:

"*Choooii*, such things you've done, booby, I want that you should meet Moses!"

Simple enough.

Until this other Bible-thumper came along. Barry Wood. Pastor of the First Baptist Church of Beverly Hills. Now, dig on that. A Cadillac agency in Beverly Hills, yes. A church, no.

He looked like Freddy Frat the super-WASP. The type who might wave a flag in one hand and his church roll in the other.

And a Baptist? Wow, everyone knows Baptists are fat and ugly black folks who roll in the aisles, get baptized once a week and wouldn't be caught dead in Beverly Hills.

I thought Barry (he liked to be called Barry) was going to shinny up that 10-foot cross when he found out I was Jewish.

"Why are you a Jew?" he asked.

"Why are you a WASP?" He didn't understand. Quite amused, I continued:

"I am . . . a Jew because I feel . . . perfectly at home at three in the morning . . . having another cup of coffee at Cantor's delicatessen."

"Wrong!" Barry jumps into the air and clicks his heels together. What is this, a true and false test?

"You call yourself Jewish because your parents are Jewish."

"Far out."

Then he did a most disgusting thing. He flipped open his Bible and it had the Old Testament! The *chutzpah*! The nerve! What is a gentile preacher who should actually be in a Cadillac agency doing with *my* book?

I had always believed the New Testament was for Christians who didn't know any better and the Old Testament was for Jews—who didn't know any better.

"Look," he says, and shows me Deuteronomy 30:6, "And the Lord thy God will circumcise thine heart." Barry said God cared about man's heart, and how it was in relation to Him, rather than ceremony.

I countered brilliantly, explaining this circumcision of the heart trip wasn't what *I* went through! He smiles. Of the *spirit*, not the flesh, he argues.

Yeah, sure. I'm glad I got it over with when I was eight days old.

"But when you were eight days old you didn't have a choice!"

Gentiles. They obviously don't know how bright

Jewish kids are. He picked up the pace.

"What does the Old Testament say about the Messiah?"

"How should I know? Maybe He'll come floating in on a cloud and feed all the starving people in China." When I was a kid my father would make me finish eating everything on my plate, reminding me about all the starving people in China.

Barry says the old Jewish leaders, hundreds of years ago, couldn't quite get it together for the Messiah. The Old Testament painted a prophetic picture of a suffering, humiliated and rejected Messiah while, at the same time, promising a reigning Messiah in His glorious kingdom.

Not satisfied with this apparently schizophrenic Anointed One of Israel, they concluded He must, in fact, be two men. Then, feeling uneasy that any king should have to go through all this misery, they edged the suffering servant out of the story and concentrated on hopes for the victorious king.

These are some Orthodox Jews beliefs. Not "Reform" Blahs.

In conclusion, he continued . . .

"Hold it! I don't want to hear anymore." Enough's enough. After all, what am I, a dummy? I'm going to listen to this WASP tell me that the leader of the gentiles is, in fact, the promised Messiah? Wow . . .

I drove home. Uneasy. My thoughts flashed back to the years spent in Sunday school at temple, hearing those great stories about Daniel being a dentist and pulling the lion's teeth; and Moses fooling everyone by walking on a sand bar when the Red Sea was at low tide.

I couldn't understand what was happening, but began to feel guilty that I always refused to take out a chick who was wearing a cross.

Yet, in spite of my affection for Arthur and Barry, I was still turned off with what they were pushing at me. I was positive I could never, in my whole life, ever say the words "Jesus Christ" without laughing and feeling sorry for the millions who believed He was something more than the world's greatest PR man.

Back to the Strip. One week. Two weeks. Three weeks. Almost every night. Arthur was smiling, laughing, praising God and not eating a thing. He'd preach, drink water or play with his new baby girl, Joy, his third child.

As my curiosity grew so did my fear of the Jewish God. Perhaps He would take revenge on me and some dark night I might be strangled by a stale bagel or drown in a sea of hot chicken soup. How could I feel attracted to something which I was sure no other Jew had ever felt drawn to?

Then this blond Baptist, Barry, filled me in on Matthew, a despised Jewish tax collector who turned in his chamber of commerce card to follow the Messiah.

And Saul of Tarsus, a member of the elite Sanhedrin and persecutor of the early Christian church, who was blinded by the Lord's light while on the road to Damascus and became a believer in the very Man he had attacked.

Only one thing was clear. My fellow Jews, modern or ancient, never give up fame or fortune to follow a long shot.

So what's with these guys? These thousands of early Christians who formed the early church? They didn't even admit they had denied their father's religion. These disciples, apostles, whatever you want to call them, and all their people depended on the *Old* Testament.

They claimed the Scripture proved this Jesus, this Dude who said such heavy things and performed all those miracles, was the Messiah *promised* by over 300 prophecies!

Barry said Daniel had predicted the date when He would be killed, Micah His birth place, Isaiah His rejection by the Jews, and on and on.

Hold it!

I was getting swept into something. A devious plot by the gentiles to take over our Jewish identity and destroy my people. No—that couldn't be it. Others had already tried.

Then what? What is it that won't let me alone?

July 22, 1969. About four weeks since Arthur held his press conference. He was down thirty pounds but just as alert and grinning as ever. He bugged me no end.

On this night Arthur asked me to pray with him. There were no others in the immediate vicinity. It was nearly 10:00 P.M., and I guessed the poor dude needed my help because he was so very weak.

Out of a generous heart I squatted by him on the sidewalk and he grasped my hand. Oh, now wait a minute! Then he bowed his head. Hey, I thought *he* needed *my* help!

So there we are, kneeling like two Holy Rollers after their evening work out. It was hot. I hoped he'd make this a quickie, because sometimes these evangelist dudes get carried away praying for everyone and everything they ever met.

Arthur thanks God for my friendship. That's cool. Then he says what a blessing it is to share God's Word, and prays that I'll ask the Messiah into my heart and receive eternal salvation claimed through the blood of the Lamb.

Now, besides a cup of coffee, eternal salvation sounded pretty good. But I'm still thinking:

Friedman, you're crazy! Kneeling on the sidewalk with a preacher talking about someone you've only been using as a swear word?

Arthur said my heart would be hardened if I postponed a decision after hearing the gospel constantly. He said I only needed to open the door a slight crack and ask the Lord to come in.

Mr. Mississippi said I only needed the faith of a grain of mustard seed (the smallest seed known 2,000 years ago) despite all the unanswered questions and doubts I had.

It was getting a little sticky. The heat crept up my back and rolled across my shoulders and under my shirt collar. I somehow sensed I'd never be able to discover a spiritual re-birth with a strictly intellectual approach but it all seemed so fantastic.

Hey! My body started shaking. Violently. My entire flesh vibrating as if from severe cold on this hot summer night. Why? What's going on?

Arthur continued to pray. I interrupted him, not being able to control myself. The words burst through my mouth and flooded the sidewalk.

"Uh . . . O.K. . . . uh, Lord . . . if You're really the Jewish Messiah then . . . ah, listen, Lord, hey . . . Jesus, yeah, Jesus, come on into my heart . . . I believe . . . come on into my life, see what You can do. Thank You for forgiving me my sins by dying for me and thanks for living in my heart."

"Whoopie!"

If Arthur had yelled any longer the Union would have given all the states back to the Confederacy. He jumped up and down, praised God and shook my already shaking hand.

After much joy from him and a stunned aftershock from me, Arthur said he'd get his building the next day, even though none were lined up.

"Why?" I asked foolishly. The evangelist said he made a deal with God: he'd stay on the Strip until I had accepted the Lord—and then God would give him a building.

The following day I covered another press conference, watching Arthur end his fast by digging into fried chicken. The building had come.

There are so many bummers in this world that the first thing we're trained to become suspicious of is a free gift. I found out eternal life can't have a price tag we can meet.

If my being born again in God's spirit, claiming what Abraham, Isaac and Jacob hoped for, was for real then I'd know about it. If this Super Dude was a figment of imagination I'd know *this* in a day or two.

What can I say? He was real! I'm still a Jew. I didn't convert to anything, just became completed in my faith. And you know, I'm glad I didn't forget what many of my Blah brothers and sisters seem to have forgotten:

When you're Jewish you should be ready for anything . . .

My Son, the Gentile

When a gentile commits himself to the Lord he will usually be met by a thump on his back or a wide yawn from his family.

When a Jew discovers the identity of his Messiah his relatives will either symbolically bury him in the family plot, force him to see the rabbi or forbid him to associate with any of his heathen friends.

If the family thinks the recently completed Jew persists in his delusions of spiritual awakening more extreme measures are in order: exiling him to an Israeli *kibbutz*, forcing him to recite his Bar Mitzvah speech into the tape recorder at least 500 times, or confiscating his credit cards.

Mother is often the most difficult person to persuade that your sanity is intact. When trying to convince her, truth is more powerful than legend; the stereotype Jewish mother might react thusly:

"Mom, count me out for dinner tonight."

"You can't make it for dinner? So who'll feed you?"

"Er, something came up. That's all."

"What am I, a stranger? Go ahead. Confide in me. Treat me like your own mother."

"Mom, it's just that . . ."

"Just what? ! All day I slave like a peasant over a hot stove so you should be happy with a full stomach. All day I prepare and wash and scrub so my Bobby will be happy."

"Maw, I'm sorry. What are you having?"

"I sent out for some chicken."

"Listen, some friends are having me over for dinner."

"How many friends?"

"About . . . eighty."

"Eighty? *Oy ga valt!* Some poor woman is cooking for eighty? Where is she serving, the Hollywood Bowl?"

"No, not quite."

"Then where?"

"Uh, at . . . church."

"Whaaa . . . ?"

"Church."

"Church! *Vey is mir.* You won't come to synagogue but you'll go to church? What happened, my son? What happened to . . . no! A *shicksa.* You met a *shicksa!*"

"No, nothing like that. I've changed. I found someone new."

"So who have you found if it's not a gentile hot-shot?"

"The . . . Messiah."

"Does He live in the neighborhood?"

"He lives everywhere."

"*Oy*. Rabbi Gluckman should hear you now. You made friends with a transient. He lives everywhere, a real bum. Better you should meet a nice *shicksa*—if she's rich."

"The Messiah, mom, has lived forever. He's . . . He's . . ."

"It's who? What's His name? This anti-Semite who's lived forever?"

"He's not anti-Semitic. He's Jewish!"

"Jewish? Does He come from a good family?"

"The best. His name is . . . *Yeshua*. Jesus. Jesus the Christ. Jesus the *Messiah*."

"I think the . . . chicken . . . has come."

"Mom, listen I . . ."

"Jeeeeeeesus? Jesus Chriiiiiiist? You're a gentile? An anti-Israeli gentile? You don't like Israel? You like the Egyptians? You want to join the country club, is that it? Listen, my son, they'll find out. They always do!"

"*He's* Jewish. *I'm* Jewish. There's no difference with me now."

"May your grandfather rest in peace, bless his heart, if he had known his grandson would do such a thing."

"I have to go, maw. I'm late."

"My son, the gentile. Late for church! Associating with gentiles and a dead man!"

"The Messiah's alive! But don't believe me. Ask Him to reveal Himself to you. He'll tell you!"

"Ask Him? A perfect stranger? *Aiii!* I've got a throbbing backache. A miserable backache. But you don't hear me complain, do you? God forbid I should complain about my backache. Hah! Ask Him, he says, a perfect stranger. Never, you hear me? I'm not so crazy as to talk to someone I can't see!"

"Bye, maw, see you later."

"Wait! Here, take a piece of chicken on the way. I wouldn't trust their cooking . . ."

Yet not all Jewish mothers would respond this way, since many have adapted themselves to modern times. For example, take this bit of conversation from a Jewish jet-setter:

"Mom, I can't stay for dinner tonight, I'm going to church."

"Don't worry about it. Dad and I are going out to eat."

"Great. Where are you going?"

"Paris."

"Paris?"

"You know Dad, sweetie, every once in a while he has this mad craving for escargot. *Fresh* escargot. Did . . . you say church?"

"Yes. I'm now a Jewish-Christian. I believe in Jesus."

"Well, drive us to the airport first, sweetie, your friend can wait."

Or how about the devoted volunteer of Hadassah?

"Mom, just thought I'd let you know I can't stay for dinner."

"The bazaar is tonight and I should worry about your dinner? Where are you going, big shot?"

"Church."

"Church?"

"I've taken the Messiah into my heart. I believe in . . ."

"Jesus! You're kidding!"

"No, mom, I . . ."

"Don't you breathe a word of this to your father!"

"Uh, I . . ."

"Or to any of my friends! *Oy,* if the Hadassah heard you went to church! Listen, you little brat, you stay out of my sight, you . . ."

"See you later."

"Far away, you traitor, this could cost me the presidency!"

Gently flowing in the stream of human compassion and humanitarian struggles for Utopia, a product of the "Get-To-Know-Your-Child" group might have the following meaningful relationship with her son:

"Mom, I can't make it for dinner tonight."

"I understand."

"I'm going to church."

"I understand."

"I believe in Jesus Christ as the Jewish Messiah."

"I understand."

"I'm a completed Jew!"

19

"I understand."

"Is that all you have to say?"

"No. Take out the trash before your father comes home."

Then, trapped in the "Think Young-Be Young" syndrome, a "teenage" matron might play the game this way:

"Mom, scratch me off the list for dinner tonight."

"Why, baby?"

"I'm going to eat dinner at church with some friends."

"That's cool."

"I believe in . . . Jesus."

"Funny you should say that, baby, 'cause your father and I were thinking about shaving our heads and chanting. Is there any difference?"

"Yes, mom. The difference between life and death."

"That's cool. Do your thing, man, but remember something."

"What's that?"

"I've got a splitting headache, so if this Jesus wants to crash here tonight the answer is 'no.' "

Church

The next night after my Messiah made me one of His saints, *without* the permission of the Vatican, I blindly appeared for my first taste of "church."

Ga valt. Wall to wall gentiles. How could I relate to these people who stood calmly in line, waiting for a mid-week dinner, without pushing, shoving or complaining their portions were too small?

I grabbed my plate and was reaching for the dollar fee when Barry threw a bill into the plate for me. First one on the house. O.K. Cool. I'd probably be assessed $10 that night for the building fund.

Then I discovered something which utterly astounded me. No dues! No DUES! Can you believe it? When my sister wished to join a temple they checked out my brother-in-law's income, credit rating and current dentist bill before deciding how much to charge him for the building fund.

At this church they had but one building. A small one. And not one person even looked at my teeth.

We sat at long tables, people slapping me on the back and several saying how they had been praying for me the past month. Believe me, they were much more excited than I was.

After dinner we filed out from the church basement and went upstairs for the service. Remarkable! No statues, giant beads, incense, neon cross, boards with nails sticking out or flying carpets.

Just rows of pews, a simple podium, stained glass window picturing you-know-who behind the choir loft (didn't look a bit Jewish) and no other adornments.

It's amazing how a common bond of faith can unite people. In spite of cultural differences. I said "can." In most cases the divergent backgrounds splinter so-called Christians into millions of spiritual toothpicks—each one trying to dig out God's meaty message in spite of the others.

As I continued to attend services, Sundays and Wednesday nights, I noticed something very peculiar. I began to grow. Not physically, mind you, although I sure could have used a little more height, but spiritually.

It's like when I got a new roommate at college. It took a while to get used to the dude's strange ("strange" means different from mine) habits, but after a while I could describe him perfectly to any who inquired.

Not so with Jesus. Christians are hard put to describe Him since many have never bothered to delve into His personality. If the Messiah knocked on their doors they'd never know who it was and would probably give Him a peanut butter sandwich, glass of water and send Him away while whispering:

"If that kid would cut his hair, take a bath and get Himself a job the good Lord might be able to make a Christian out of Him!"

Good Lord.

Anyway, after the months passed it became evident our church membership was undergoing a change. More and more Jewish youth accepted His light and joined our ranks, immediately indoctrinating our gentile brothers into the mysteries of the Jewish soul.

This took as much wind out of the straight, Bible-belt Midwesterners as when they first had to share a pew with a long-haired Christian named "Sunny" or "Drifter."

Before you get the wrong idea I better set you straight. Mine was a most remarkable church. We had the oldies-but-goodies and the teeny-boppers, the conservative businessmen, clean-cut college kids, unemployed artists, unemployed actors, unemployed actresses and a general assortment of the undefinable unemployed.

Yet we survived. Another promise, right? Right. The Lord said if we'd trust Him He'd supply all our needs. He's never failed yet. So a nucleus of men, financially blessed, supported most of our budget.

Most churches are *not* operated this way. Most

ignore God's promises, and God, for fear of scaring off a doctor, lawyer or—because of recent pressure by minority groups—an Indian chief.

Most churches erect a giant building if three people miss Sunday school two weeks in a row. Gotta keep that head count up . . .

Most churches appoint deacons who are self-employed and thereby able to play volleyball for two hours each afternoon.

Most churches have pastors who try so hard to make a name for themselves in the community that their Bible remains buried under a pile of lists for "good prospects," "good business contacts," "good songs for the church talent show," "good speaking engagements for good donations," and hundreds of visitors' cards which they *must* get around to.

But I digress.

Two months after my sidewalk completion I felt moved to declare openly to my brothers and sisters what had taken place within me. So—I decided to be baptized.

Hold it! None of that! You think you know what this means, right? Just like *I* thought before I knew. Not so, man, not so. It is simply an act of obedience to one of the Lord's commands. He didn't make many. Baptism declares:

"Hey, you sitting out there on the outside! Guess what all has a-happened to me in the inside?"

Simple enough. An immersion in water to symbolize being buried with the Messiah into death, and then rising again from the water to symbolize His resurrection—and our spiritual resurrection—into a new life.

So what happens. Of all nights I'm to be dunked —on the eve of Yom Kippur, the Day of Atonement.

"*Aiiiiiiiii!*" my sister screams over the phone, "can't you talk to a rabbi? TALK TO A RABBI!" (sob . . . sob . . . sneeze). "I can't believe it. What have they done to you?"

Explaining in the midst of a deluge of tears doesn't work at all. I let her continue.

"I don't want my children growing up knowing that their . . . their uncle believes . . . Jesus rose from the dead!"

The Bible would call her a Sadducee, not believing in the resurrection of the dead. I would simply call her hysterical.

My family boycotted my baptism. Nonetheless the great event was attended by the same photographer who first covered Arthur's story with me. Although he wasn't a believer, the seriousness of the ritual prompted him to prepare me in a somber, respectful way.

Just as I headed for the old tank in a make-shift baptistry he handed me a snorkel and swim fins.

Not to be outdone, I stood in waist-deep water and, when Barry asked me why I wanted to be baptized, I answered in twenty-five thousand words or less as I delivered a lengthy sermon on my "completion."

It wasn't until some time later that I discovered most persons quickly express a faith in the Lord in one or two sentences. I had a perfect excuse, though. I was the first person I had seen get baptized.

During the following months I became slowly welded into a family of assorted persons who shared problems, joy, money, happiness, frustrations and victories. Kind of like an Establishment commune.

The membership fluctuated. New people constantly replaced the old as young Christians stayed long enough to grow out of their spiritual diapers before hitching home to show friends how God had redecorated their old self.

When church members from another town wished to join they would often have a former pastor send a note to our church acknowledging their transfer.

Not realizing Jewish "churches" just don't operate this way, a well-meaning gentile asked one of our Hebrew brothers:

"Oh! Did your temple send a letter?"

A letter, yet. The rabbi wouldn't even bother to drop gefilte fish into the church collection plate as a protest . . .

Bob Friedman and Jesus

It is only after I became a believer in the Messiah that I began to reflect upon my past life in an attempt to discover if God had been dealing with me. Suddenly certain events flashed through my memory banks and I imagined God's voice reverberating:

"Ah, ha! So you think I've left you alone, eh?"

Then I had to admit I had always been plagued with a nagging knowledge of this Jesus. A sort of seriocomedy of Bob Friedman and Jesus. Me first. Him—away back there in the shadows.

I was born in San Francisco on September 4, 1943, and seriously doubt if my presence had any effect whatsoever on the outcome of the war. At the age of two, before my legs had gotten used to the

Bay City's hills, my family moved to Los Angeles.

In 1950 we shifted our belongings to my parents' present home in Santa Monica. A gentile neighborhood with a smattering of Jews. Like finding a few good rye breads amidst hundreds of loaves of white.

My oldest sister Judy and I were the real "Jews" of the family, taking our faith more seriously than my parents or two other sisters, Linda and Pam. But I'll hit you with the consequences of this a little later.

Meanwhile—at Roosevelt Grammar School. At Christmastime the entire class was forced to participate in a program of carols, but I refused to sing about a little baby who chewed straw for his pacifier. Being the shortest kid in the class, I stood in the front, not making a sound, but moving my mouth in hopes of fooling the teacher.

Come to think of it, maybe she wasn't fooled. At one time I had wanted to learn to play the violin but was quickly refused. I couldn't sing "Three Blind Mice" on key.

This was ridiculous. It was just a new key, that's all. Instead of rewarding me for my inventive talents in the world of music they simply concluded I was the most horrible singer in modern history.

Dozens of people have since confirmed this, but what does that prove? I still think it's a completely new key.

I had inherited my inventive abilities from my father. When he was fourteen he dreamed up the self-winding wrist watch, but didn't know what to do with it. Years later he sold the "clear" cartridge idea to Sheaffer's so users of fountain pens could determine how much ink remained.

Yet although he invented dozens of practical and commercial things he seemed satisfied to stay with his baby: a corrugated drinking tube, called the Flex-Straw, which became an instant success with hospitals as well as housewives.

When I was very young we did have a Christmas tree. As a thing of beauty. It smells good, right? Yet after I began attending Sunday school and learning a thing or two I refused to let that pagan symbol into our home.

Pam was heartbroken. She loved trees. Linda loved trees as long as they were still in the ground on a mountain slope, while my parents were apathetic. Judy was on my side and we won out. No tree.

Like good Jewish families everywhere we celebrated Chanukah and its feast of lights. I really enjoyed this and made sure the whispering and jokes had ceased before saying the Hebrew prayer over the candles.

Although I was very serious about it, the last two words of the prayer are ". . . shel Chanukah" and it was difficult for me not to think of a gas station.

At Sunday school we'd goof off with the other kids and avoid the rabbi. We assumed he had a horrible sense of humor. The Bible stories were only that—stories. Once in a while our teacher would interject a scientific explanation for a biblical miracle.

Never, never, in this reform temple did anyone mention a *personal* God. A God who cared about us, loved us, took care of us and knew when we passed notes behind the teacher's back.

My parents went to temple very seldom. My father was raised in an Orthodox home and he had received his quota of religion at an early age. God was not a subject we discussed at home, due to indifference rather than hostility.

Yet each year we held a Passover seder for the family. Lamb shank. Hard-boiled egg. Parsley The whole works. Dad would tediously go through the Haggadah, the book outlining the service, although in later years not enough members of our group had the patience for a seder so it was given up.

How could I blame them? It did seem a bit foolish to force yourself to go through a ritual because it was expected of you. One year Pam had almost put the finishing blow on the entire scene.

It's customary to "open the door" for Elijah, the great Jewish prophet who someday would announce the coming of the Messiah. For many Orthodox Jews this is a very real hope.

We hadn't noticed Pam was missing from the table. Then, when the door for Elijah was opened, she came walking in with a towel draped over her head and her teeth clamped tight to muffle the giggles.

I was furious! This was a crushing blow to my efforts to have a respectable seder.

After being graduated from high school I served in the army reserve for six months' active duty at Ft. Ord, California, near Monterey.

Wow, man. Here come the Southerners. My first

exposure to those folks I had just seen in movies.

"Hey, man, how do ya spell stamp?" one asked me.

"Stamp?"

"Yeah, uh, huh."

"S - T - A - M - P - Q."

"P - Q?"

"Yeah, uh, huh."

"Thanks, man."

Of course these dudes weren't the cream of the Dixie brain trust, but as far as I knew they were. Immediately I saw one wearing a cross and concluded it was necessary to commit intellectual suicide to become a Christian.

All the other gentiles, or Christians as I thought, who had a little something going for them upstairs yet still went to church must have ulterior motives. To recruit for the Elks Club, maybe.

It was a definite advantage to have "Jewish" stamped on your dog tags since this meant we received three three-day passes during the High Holy Days. A Catholic friend was infuriated when I told him I was going to get another pass for Cha-*noo*-kah.

If I had pronounced Chanukah correctly it would have lost something of its humorous impact.

After a year and a half at San Diego State, during which time I made horrible grades, I decided to take a break and work in San Francisco for a while.

My educational achievements were always disappointing. I rebelled against my parents' pushing me to get good marks, so considered it a real challenge to see how well I could do on tests with no study time under my belt.

In high school I had made straight A's in math and had done well in science and English classes— due strictly to my ability to pick things up quickly in class (not because I actually sat down on my *own* time and studied!).

San Diego State had wanted me to take all those advanced courses for the "elite" after I finished in the top two percent of their entrance examination, but I declined. Work harder? Forget it.

I stumbled from semester to semester with no real purpose other than that of obtaining a piece of paper my father could hang on his wall under those of my three sisters. They had all been graduated from U.C.L.A.

In San Francisco I got a "job" selling encyclopedias door to door. My income for three weeks was a promising zero. Lot of potential, though, lot of potential.

The last home I went to was occupied by a young couple with a small baby. I'm a sucker for kids. When I saw their meager surroundings I told them the last thing they needed was an encyclopedia and they should save up for the child.

So, I'm a lousy salesman. Big deal. Anyway, I beat out ten applicants at a legal publishing firm and became a "correspondent." I wrote attorneys and told them to cool it 'cause the volume they ordered was unavoidably detained in the elevator or something.

Both the correspondent next to me and myself were quick workers. She was from the coal country of Minnesota, a real doll, and we became close friends. People would often stare at us; why, I don't know, as we held hands and skipped down Market Street.

I'm all of five feet four inches tall and she was a mere five feet eleven and a half.

We'd write jokes and poems back and forth all day long. Many of these concerned life and God, since this same nagging kept intruding on my privacy. Why? What? Who? When? Huh?

Once I found myself in a serious frame of mind and wrote:

> Up above this dreary fort
> Lurks a place of last resort—
> Headed by a weird creation,
> A figment of man's imagination.
>
> "We want answers!" masses scream,
> So they receive a mystic dream—
> Super-nature in all its glory,
> Like a child's fairy story.
>
> Six days, brother, and then man,
> That is how this world began—
> So now please pray and do pretend
> We know not how this world will end.

I also carried in my wallet a definition of God which said people take all the questions they haven't discovered answers to, wrap them up into a big bundle, kick it out into space and call it "God" to ease their minds.

Man, after all, had certainly created God in his image.

In San Francisco I lived with a few guys attending San Francisco State. We had an old house in a white and black neighborhood near campus. Once in a while I'd sneak down to the corner while a black church was in session and groove on those soul sounds pouring out into the street.

After four months in San Francisco I returned to San Diego State. At the time there was one long-haired student on campus. Most pointed to him, cracked jokes and let him sit alone in a corner of the cafeteria.

I really never dated a great deal, since I didn't particularly care for Jewish girls and the gentile chicks were heavy into their sorority scene.

I had had the misfortune of meeting Jewish girls in Los Angeles who were so wrapped up in the world of materialism that the only thing they could relate to was where daddy was going to build another home or what country they wanted to buy after graduating.

While I was still a teenager, one (she was poor) told me:

"Why, when you turn sixteen you either get a new car or a nose job!" Many get both.

The gentile chicks I met at college were on an equally bad trip. This was before the taking of drugs, let's-capture-a-building days. They held on to their image of Sally Sorority.

"Hi, there, I'm Sally Sorority! Look at my pin!" (giggles); "Oh, wow, I just love all my sisters so much!" (giggles); "Are you going to take me out tonight? Ummm? To a swingin' place? Ummm? Are we going alone?" (giggles).

"No. We're bringing your housemother."

"Oh."

Out of periodic loneliness I went a couple of times to a reform Jewish temple in San Diego. After the service I carefully nibbled on a piece of cake during the *oneg shabbat*, the social hour.

No one said hello to me.

In the summer of 1965 I was a counselor at a resident camp in Idyllwild, California, a restful mountain resort town. It was an Orthodox camp and I rather enjoyed dressing up for Friday night services and eating good Jewish chicken and matzo ball soup.

Yet, once again, it all seemed so surfacy. Nothing would reach into your guts and shake you up. Nothing from out of this world to be offered as an alternative to society's plan. Just—nothing.

When registering each semester at college we had an option as to whether we wanted to fill in the space labeled "religion." This meant if I put down "Jewish" the ethnic social group, Hillel, would be on my back all year and too many of their members reminded me of third assistant tailors from New York's garment district.

I wrote down, "Friedmanism."

"What's Friedmanism?" the girl collecting the cards would ask.

"Friedmanism," I informed her, "is the only religion which can save Jesus Christ."

I thought this very clever. A cute twist. Yet every time I said it something down deep bothered me. Bad vibes. But I ignored them.

With two years to go I still hadn't settled on a

major. I flipped through the school catalogue and found out there was no language requirement for journalism majors. Whamo. I'm in.

Writing had always been my favorite hobby. I seriously thought of becoming a writer when in high school but my parents discouraged me.

"Do you know how many starving writers there are?"

I could imagine.

Yet I wanted to get through college. My father at last conceded I might be able to snag a job with a major in journalism, so didn't argue too much.

I loved it. Really far out. I even covered the student council meetings (as befits the ace reporter) and shook up the school establishment.

Each member of student government was a Greek, a frat man or sorority chick. To rub a little dirt into their neatly pressed clothes I'd show up to cover a meeting wearing bermudas, a ripped T-shirt, army fatigue jacket, bare feet and a big cigar smoking away.

If they said anything I made them look like idiots in the paper's lead story the next day. This wasn't too difficult to do.

After being graduated from good old State in June, 1967, I worked on a legal newspaper in Los Angeles for the summer. Two of my brothers-in-law are attorneys and law sounded fairly challenging.

I took the national law school admissions test, finished in the top fifteen percent and applied for law school. I felt pretty good having done so well against Harvard, Yale and the Oklahoma Military Academy.

I was accepted at a few schools, but thoughts of burying my nose into 1,000-page books for three years kept plaguing me. You know, the only dude around with white skin during the summer—Coke-bottle glasses—telling Orange County residents it's time to take down their "IMPEACH EARL WARREN" signs.

I passed on law school.

My fall of 1967 was spent in Europe, including a brief visit to Israel. I went by myself, a graduation present from my Aunt Betty, but didn't enjoy the rainy days and lack of company.

In Israel I noticed smoke pouring into my room in the middle of night. Looking out the window in a half-dazed stupor, I saw flames. Sluggishly I worked my way downstairs, woke up a sleeping night clerk and asked him to quit burning garbage until the next day.

He panicked. The "garbage" was the hotel. The place was on fire!

I also picked apples on a kibbutz for a week. We'd ride out to the orchard in a one-horse cart with a grizzled old Sabra (native Israeli) in charge. The two of us sat on a make-shift car seat fastened to the flat, wooden wagon.

He turned his head to talk to one of the others riding with us and handed me the reins with no word of explanation. Hmmmm. A horse, right?

It slowed to a walk, having confirmed its suspicions that an amateur was in charge. Not wishing to be outdone I slapped the reins hard against its side and screamed.

"EEEEEEE-YAAA!"

Va-room! It took off like a shot and nearly bounced me off. It was then I heard the only words I ever understood from this head apple-picker. He slowly turned to face me and grinned:

"Ben Hur!"

Several Israelis informed me they were the most irreligious people in the world. They were proud of it! They knew the history of the Bible, having studied it in school, but they lacked the touch of God and missed God's plan for the Jews.

This is due in part to the fact only the Orthodox branch of Judaism is recognized. The Reform and Conservative movements are not tolerated, thereby forcing energetic youngsters to shun Judaism completely rather than succumb to a rigid religious life.

My deeply implanted feelings that God, if He existed, must desire *something* from us were aroused by the negative reaction of the Israelis to any heaven-bound obligation. I admire and respect with a deep love what they have done with the land, but their souls are still desert wastes.

Back to the states. Back to the ho-hum world. Back to being a newspaper reporter.

I worked for Copley Newspapers, an extremely conservative group, for the first nine months of 1968. Most of the time was spent with the Glendale *News-Press.*

The action of a reporter was stimulating, the slow hours were unbearable and the routine often got musty. One of our editors, Ted Mutch, had been trained through the fire of English journalism and taught me what I could never have learned in school.

As far as the community went, I was a very round peg trying to fit into a very, very square hole.

It appeared most of the town was owned and operated, if only indirectly, by church people. I'd cover one or more of their events, observe their people and conclude:

1. Christians had crew-cuts.

2. Christians always voted Republican.

3. Christians could do a lot of good, like building hospitals and orphanages, but always seemed individually detached.

4. Some Christians kept shotguns under their beds in case the Commies snuck in during the night or "those" people tried to move in next door.

The newspaper had an office in La Crescenta, in the foothills, and there worked an extremely sweet woman who admitted she believed the Bible was literally true. Man, can you believe it? Myself and another employe hassled this person without mercy, ripping her to shreds with our sarcastic tongues.

If only she could see me now.

I quit, moved to Santa Monica and decided I was a free-lance writer. By the end of the year I was desperate for a job after experiencing the *famine* part of the business without getting in on the *feast* part.

Back to newspaper work. This time for a short stint at the *Herald-Examiner.* After about five months those old fears crept back. Where ya headed, kid? Hey, man, will you die with a gold watch in your hand for thirty years' faithful service? Is *that* all life is about?

I floated from day to day. Once in a while a bottle of Scotch resting on my kitchen shelf would help me "unwind" at night after I had finished a midnight shift. Before I had a chance to change my life's direction again my city editor sent me to the Sunset Strip to find out what this evangelist was up to.

You know the rest. Bob Friedman and Jesus.

Just think. After all those years we finally met.

The Twelve-Year-Old Mench
(Smart and Spunky)

Right from the beginning there was something very unusual about this child Jesus. You are all familiar with standard Christmas-type stories about stars, wise men and stables, but the best part takes place in the great Temple in Jerusalem.

After eight days Jesus was circumcised according to the Law of Moses, for Joseph and Mary adhered to the Law very diligently. Then they recalled something else the Lord had said to Moses:

"Sanctify to me every first-born, the first offspring of every womb among the sons of Israel, both of man and beast; it belongs to me" (Exod. 13:2).

So off to Jerusalem they went to present this first-born son to God and to present a sacrifice for

Mary's purification according to the Lord's Word in Exodus: "a pair of turtledoves or two young pigeons."

Today the secretary of the Sisterhood would merely ask for a "reasonable donation" to encourage the women's projects in Sunday school and help support the "First Annual Beth Mishigas Talent Show."

But back to the Temple . . .

It seems when Jesus was brought as a baby to Jerusalem there was a dude hanging around whose name was Simeon. He was a very righteous and devout Jew, devoted to his people, and very much in love with God.

It is written that old Simeon received a message from the Lord promising he would see God's Christ, or Messiah, before he would see death.

When Simeon glanced at Mary's baby he knew. Snatching the child into his own arms he didn't say, "Kitchee koo" or "Is it a boy or a girl?" but simply declared:

"Now Lord, Thou dost let Thy bondservant depart in peace, according to Thy word; For mine eyes have seen Thy salvation, which Thou hast prepared in the presence of all peoples, a light of revelation to the gentiles, and the glory of Thy people Israel" (Luke 2:29-32).

That was a mouthful. Simeon is saying this tiny kid wrapped up in a bundle is the hope of Israel, the Messiah, who's going to give a fair shake to both Jew and gentile.

Joseph and Mary blew their minds as Simeon continued to tell Mary this very child had been appointed for the fall and rise of many in Israel.

The Temple was bigger than the Vatican and some persons could stay there day and night without being kicked out for loitering. Such a person was Hannah.

Hannah was the daughter of Phanuel, if that makes it clearer for you, of the tribe of Asher. She was eighty-four at the time the baby Jesus was being rocked by Simeon. For days and nights she had been praying and fasting and was known to be a great prophetess.

Just as Simeon finished doing his thing old Hannah crept up and took over. She gave thanks to God and pointed to Jesus as the hope of all those looking for the redemption of Jerusalem.

Satisfied that their son was no ordinary boy, Mary and Joseph returned to Galilee and the city of Nazareth.

Every year they took their family to Jerusalem for the Passover. This was the time of year when all the Jews thanked God for delivering them from Egypt, set up business deals and exchanged recipes for chocolate-covered matzos.

By the time Jesus was twelve there was a large group of friends and relatives returning to Nazareth after the feast. His parents were unaware He stayed behind in Jerusalem and probably figured Jesus was off somewhere in the caravan playing with His brother Jimmy.

After a day's journey it became obvious Jesus was missing when He didn't show up for dinner again.

"*Oy,*" Joseph said, "Jesus is late. And you know how He hates cold blintzes."

After more time they began searching for Him among their relatives and friends. When they couldn't find Him they made a U-turn with the family donkey and headed back for Jerusalem.

Three days passed as Joseph and Mary hunted everywhere for their oldest boy. Shops, homes, countryside, everywhere. Then, much to their surprise, they found Him.

In Temple. Rapping with the rabbis, the cantors, and the officers of the Temple youth group.

"Such a bright boy!" the elders said. "Such wisdom! Where does He get all the answers?" Jesus kind of looked up at them and smiled:

"You'd never believe it . . ."

About now Mary pulls Him by the ear and complains.

"Son, why have You done this to us? We've been searching frantically for You!" Then Jesus really lays a heavy line on her:

"Why is it that you were looking for Me? Did you not know that I had to be in My Father's house?"

Mary, Joseph and the others scratched their heads because they couldn't figure out what He was talking about. After all, it wasn't Joseph's house—he could never afford to make a down payment on something as huge as the Temple.

But Jesus was talking about His real daddy—God. And for a Jewish youth to call God "Father" was a crime against the anti-defamation league.

But, being an obedient son, the Messiah followed His parents home. He was the only one who knew His fantastic knowledge was prophesied in Isaiah, chapter 11:

"Then a shoot will spring from the stem of Jesse, and a branch from his roots will bear fruit. And the Spirit of the Lord will rest on Him, the spirit of wisdom and understanding, the spirit of counsel and strength, the spirit of knowledge and the fear of the LORD (vv. 1,2).

So when He was twelve years old the Messiah dazzled the elders with His brilliant light of truth from His Father. The same light that shone from His eyes shines today. It's the same light that captured my curiosity—and then my heart.

And if the Temple big shots in the Messiah's day had realized what this light, this wisdom, was all about they never, *never* would have told this brilliant kid He'd have to be bar mitzvahed in order to become a man.

California Freaks

This is the story about Sam Rivers. Sam was really cool. Sam was a bit of everything that comes to California: drifter, doper, ex-Vietnam veteran, ex-student, ecology freak, white defender of minority groups and vociferous hater of General Motors.

He used to be heavy into dope. Sam would trip out for so long that when he'd crash it'd be like staying awake and when he was awake it'd be just like crashing.

This twenty-year-old had hitched all over America. Crawling through the Deep South, walking high in San Francisco or running for his life outside Jackson Hole, Wyoming.

Sam had done it all. Acid. Downers. Uppers. Speed. A little smack. Chicks. Everything. One day he decided there wasn't *any* place he hadn't been and *nothing* he hadn't tried to escape from all those places he had been.

It was time for another change. Sam caught a ride to the Strip, also known as Sunset Boulevard in West Hollywood, and there decided to stay away from drugs completely in search of a more permanent high which was a whole lot less expensive.

As soon as he hit the street he was approached by two long-hairs who thrust a piece of paper at him and glared with a self-righteous vengeance. Sam blinked under the silent attack and read what was written on the paper:

"You're going to hell!"

So what else is new? He started to hand the paper back but they refused to accept it.

"Hey, man, you're damned! You're a sinner! You've been condemned! C'mon, get on our bus and we'll get your head together with Jesus!"

They took his arm and started leading him to an old school bus which was painted with various slogans telling of God's wrath. Sam pulled his arm away and begged off.

"Look, freaks, go do your thing, but count me out."

"You can't be serious! What's your name?"

"This week?"

"Don't kid around with God's children, man, or the Lord will take His revenge!"

Sam whistled under his breath and shoved the paper into one of their shirt pockets. Laughing as he walked backwards away from them, Sam shook his head and yelled out a parting remark.

"Hey, you freaks must have missed something that even *I* heard about once."

"What's that?" they snarled.

"God is love!"

Man, what a trip. None of that crazy Jesus stuff for Sam. There were enough bummers in the world without getting threatened by more. If those guys were going to heaven Sam would just as soon not be there.

He walked down the Strip, peering into a corner pool hall, past "head" shops selling incense, leather vests and the latest book from India's famous guru culture. Once in a while a hip-looking dude would ask if he needed something but Sam dismissed the offer with a laugh.

What he needed he couldn't find, but he'd know when he found it.

A bright green neon sign grabbed his attention and Sam read "MEDITATION—IT WORKS" before noticing they offered love, peace, and all the other goodies most people were looking for. Willing to try anything, Sam went inside.

A tall dark-haired girl was obviously disagreeing with another girl behind the counter. The representative was calm, unexcitable and trying to be pleasant. Her "client" was super uptight.

"Do you know I've sunk all kinds of money into this stinking place and nothing has happened yet. What do you . . ."

"Hey! Did you drop something?" the calm one asked. "Are you getting bad vibes from something you dropped?"

"Hell, no!" the tall girl screamed, "I'm getting bad vibes from the bread you cats ripped off me!"

The one behind the counter saw Sam for the first time and attempted to look past the thrashing arms to question the new arrival.

"Yes, may I help you?"

"Hold it!" the furious girl interrupted, "I'm not through with you yet! I want back every cent, every single *cent* you cats took me for! Eighteen hundred bucks and I haven't even been to the moon! I'll be back. Believe me, I'll be back!"

The girl whipped past Sam and stormed out of the place, slamming the door so hard it took a few seconds for the glass to quit rattling in the front window. The remaining girl smiled as if nothing had happened.

"Yes, may I help you now?"

"Thanks anyway."

With his bedroll strapped tightly on his back, Sam stuck out his thumb and waited for a ride to take him away from this hypocritical center of commercial anti-Establishmentarianism. He waited. And waited. And waited.

Finally a VW bus stopped for him and Sam climbed in. The smiling driver was stoned. Really high. And, to Sam's amazement, this cat was turned on to something Sam had never tried. A natural, eternal high.

The driver said he was turned on to Jesus.

"Let me out!" Sam yelled and reached for the door handle. The van was speeding along and couldn't stop in the flow of traffic, but the driver said he'd oblige when he could.

"I've just been with some of your people," Sam exploded, "and I'm not ready for any more threats, damnations or finger-pointing!"

"Do you see me doing that?"

"You will."

"Not likely. The Lord loves you. He doesn't want to scare you to death. Did you meet some people on the street?"

"Yeah."

"Well, they were probably off and running on another kind of trip. As far as I'm concerned there's too much to the real Truth to ever want to isolate one little point and warp it beyond recognition."

Sam was a kid when his old lady tried to shove him down some smelly church aisle. Sam didn't buy it. Then he kicked up a fuss and stormed out of church and the next Sunday his parents dragged him to another building in town 'cause they were too embarrassed to go back to the old one.

The people weren't any different in the new place, Sam remembered. They scraped their chins on the ground, bragged about what they had done for God and told him to wear a tie (Sam that is, not God).

"Stick with me for a half hour," the driver said, "I'll take you somewhere that'll blow your mind."

It's not every day you can have your mind blown free of charge. Sam agreed.

As they drove, the driver explained he had been into an organic food trip, trying to generate power from within by living a pure, natural life and eating only raw, natural food.

After a few months of organic honey, wheat germ, soy beans and various vegetables he wound up twenty pounds lighter with indigestion, heart burn and a mad craving for a rare steak.

The van pulled into the parking lot of a modern looking church. Sam said he had tried that trip as a kid, but the driver just grinned and encouraged him to stay for at least a few minutes. O.K. Why not?

Sam's mind was definitely blown. So where are the old ushers? The huge collection plates? The little old ladies who gossiped during the sermon or the sign-up sheet for a church retreat?

All he saw were *at least* a thousand teenagers and dudes in their early twenties . . . uh, what can he say? . . . uh, praising God! That's it, they were praising God! Sitting in pews or sitting cross-legged on the carpet, they praised God!

Weird. Really weird.

Here's what was missing with those other freaks. Here was love. And you didn't have to crawl into some dirty bus and head out for nowhere.

Here's what Scientology missed. What these cats had was so precious that the only price tag had been paid by another many centuries ago.

Here's what organic food missed. The power, boldness and peace bubbling from these kids tapped an unlimited source—without any recipes.

Sam stayed for hours. He had found it. And after he stuck it out and learned more and more about the Man who had changed him so much, Sam Rivers came to a shocking conclusion:

For the first time in his life he trusted someone over thirty.

My Mother, the Gentile

The man which we are about to discuss was born in Ur of the land of the Chaldeans. His mother, a status quo gentile, worshiped idols, baked bread and occasionally nagged Terah, her husband.

The wife of our hero was named Sarai, the founder of Planned Parenthood—even though at the time she couldn't have had a child if she had wanted one.

After Terah had died at the tender age of 205, his son received instructions as to what he was to do. Not orders from the cleaners-of-the-idols or the sweepers-of-the-statues, but real, authentic commands from God Himself.

Yes, our hero whose mother bowed down to sticks and stones was none other than good old Abram. The name he receives later in this Genesis account will be much more familiar to you.

But back to the Lord who stopped Abram in his tracks and said:

"Go forth from your country, and from your relatives and from your father's house, to the land which I will show you; and I will make you a great nation, and I will bless you, and make your name great;

"And so you shall be a blessing; and I will bless those who bless you, and the one who curses you I will curse. And in you all the families of the earth shall be blessed" (Gen. 12:1-3).

Presto. Instant father of my ancestors. The first Jew.

It's obvious Abram's love for a one, true God prompted the Lord to lay such heavy promises on him, since Abram did nothing in a physical sense to earn such things.

So at the age of seventy-five Abram took Sarai and his nephew Lot, packed up three sets of camel-hair luggage and journeyed to Canaan, where the Lord promised the land to Abram's descendants.

In the following stories Lot splits for another land, Abram panics, passes off Sarai as his sister, loses her for a while to an Egyptian pharaoh and then is promised by God to have an heir through Sarai.

When Abram expressed reasonable doubt as to this, God took Abram outside his tent and said:

"Now look toward the heavens, and count the

stars, if you are able to count them. . . . So shall your descendants be" (Gen. 15:5).

Then the Old Testament says Abram believed in the Lord; and God reckoned it to Abram as righteousness. Just because he believed. That's not asking much from someone who's going to have so many kids that he'd never be able to carry all their pictures in his wallet.

After Abram had lived ten years in Canaan his wife shrugged her shoulders and offered up her Egyptian maid Hagar as another wife to her husband. Believe me, Sarai was no spring chicken.

The consequences of this were tremendous. Abram was eighty-six years old when Hagar bore him a son, but listen to what the Lord said to Hagar about this new soul before she had given birth:

"Behold, you are with child, and you shall bear a son; and you shall call his name Ishmael, because the Lord has given heed to your affliction. And he will be a wild ass of a man, his hand will be against everyone, and everyone's hand will be against him; and he will live to the east of all his brothers" (Gen. 16:11,12).

Presto. Instant enemy of my ancestors. The first Arab.

But can you imagine? People coming up to Hagar and asking what she thought her child would be like and all she can do is say:

"Oh, I reckon he's going to be a wild ass of a man."

Ishmael had just become a teenager when, at the age of ninety-nine, the LORD appeared to Abram and, without any papers filed in court or legal hokey-pokey, He changed his name.

This was *not* for business reasons, since Abram was doing quite well, thank you. This was for *eternal* reasons, which of course many can't relate to when they get up in the morning. You won't find most men digging into scrambled eggs, smiling at their wife and declaring:

"Wow, honey! Doesn't the thought of eternal things make you tingle all over?"

But I digress.

God changed his name from Abram, which means "exalted father," to Abraham, which means "father of a multitude." Then the Lord added:

"And I will establish My covenant between Me and you and your descendants after you throughout their generations for an everlasting covenant, to be God to you and to your descendants after you" (Gen. 17:7).

It had a certain permanent ring about it . . .

Now, *after* Abraham believed God, the Lord instituted circumcision of the flesh to symbolize the covenant. Every male in Abraham's household was circumcised that day, including Ishmael, who at the time had no idea that one day his descendants wouldn't let people into his lands without a baptism certificate.

After this God once again reminded Abraham he would have an heir. Abraham could barely muster enough energy to mend a tent or play a few hands of poker with the shepherd.

"Then God said to Abraham, 'As for Sarai your

wife, you shall not call her name Sarai, but Sarah (princess) shall be her name.

" 'And I will bless her, and indeed I will give you a son by her. Then I will bless her, and she shall be a mother of nations; kings of peoples shall come from her.'

"Then Abraham fell on his face and laughed, and said in his heart, 'Will a child be born to a man one hundred years old? And will Sarah, who is ninety years old, bear a child?' " (Gen. 17:17).

You have to agree it sounded ridiculous.

Sarah lived to the age of 127, long enough to see her son Isaac grow to manhood after his miraculous birth in spite of Abraham's wavering faith.

You might think Abraham would leave his tired bones alone, but instead he kept a good thing going. After Sarah was buried he waited a respectable time, then—used to having someone around the tent—he married Keturah.

In case names like Bill, George, Ted and such seem too common for you, next time you have a baby you might follow Abraham and Keturah's lead and name your sons Zimran, Jokshan, Medan, Midian, Ishbak or Shuah.

Well, maybe not Ishbak . . .

To wrap up this story of a son of a gentile who became the first Jew through the grace of God, Genesis says:

"And these are all the years of Abraham's life that he lived, one hundred and seventy-five years.

"And Abraham breathed his last and died in a ripe old age, an old man and satisfied with life; and he was gathered to his people" (Gen. 25:7,8).

The history, culture and accomplishments of my people are utterly amazing, and I'm glad the average Jewish youth has an opportunity to become refined, gentle, calm, strong and intelligent like our great father Abraham.

For if God hadn't chosen this believing man to begin our nation, a ten-year-old Jewish kid today might receive this type of tongue-lashing from his mother:

"Play, play! All you want to do is play! Clean up your room, turn off the T.V. and dust the idols, *then* you can play!"

Matthew Six

The first Jewish-Christians were a pretty tight group of believers who basically had one faith in one God through one Messiah. Such questions as "Should we let the gentiles in on this?" were answered and they happily formed groups of brothers and sisters who worshiped together, ate together and shared their spiritual goodies together.

Then, as hundreds of years of man's ego crept in, something quite foreign to the first believers invaded their whole scene. Denominations.

Methodists, Catholics, Episcopalians, Baptists, Presbyterians and all the rest are *not* mentioned in the Bible due to the fact God didn't want to encourage individual hang-ups.

In all fairness, some relgious groups were created to counter others which threw away the Bible in favor of philosophy texts, "self esteem" manuals or the latest publication from the Department of Motor Vehicles.

But imagine, if you will, what would happen if the Lord zipped into one of our monster churches today and—amidst the glamor, glitter and organization—attempt to deliver the same message He did in the sixth chapter of Matthew.

"Welcome to our church," a deacon would say to Him after the service, "we're happy to have you. In fact, *many* of our people have, uh, long hair. Of course, they *are* younger.

"I'd like you to meet the pastor. He's a fine man. We've been friends for years and worked together at our mission. We've spent long hours in prayer together—on our knees mind you—and I'm terribly proud of how the Lord has humbled us."

"Beware of practicing your righteousness before men to be noticed by them; otherwise you have no reward with your Father who is in heaven."

"Huh? None of us seeks reward! We give! Take Joe over there, he gave fifty bucks for our camp fund, and Chuck pitched in a hundred fifty—of course, he wouldn't miss it much. Then Mike promised another twenty-five and . . ."

"When therefore you give alms, do not sound a trumpet before you, as the hypocrites do in the synagogues and in the streets, that they may be honored by men. Truly I say to you, they have their reward in full.

"But when you give alms, do not let your left

hand know what your right hand is doing; that your alms may be in secret; and your Father who sees in secret will repay you."

"Sounds familiar, sir, yes, that sounds familiar. Have you ever been trained? Very important, you know. You need to be trained in how to be led by the Spirit. Very important. Say, why not come to a prayer meeting tonight? Man! The last one went on for five hours and thirteen minutes! Power! That's power!"

"And when you pray, you are not to be as the hypocrites; for they love to stand and pray in the synagogues, and on the street corners, in order to be seen by men. Truly I say to you, they have their reward in full.

"But you, when you pray, go into your inner room, and when you have shut your door, pray to your Father who is in secret, and your Father who sees in secret will repay you.

"And when you are praying, do not use meaning-less repetition, as the gentiles do, for they suppose that they will be heard for their many words."

"Gentiles? What do you think *we* are? Listen, you're not one of them . . . no, you can't be. As I always say, friend, if the good Lord wanted us to mix with all them others He never would have put some in that bad part of town and others in that snobby section where they just eat smelly food all day. No sir, we spend our time praying for *good* folk."

"Therefore do not be like them; for your Father knows what you need, before you ask Him. Pray, then, in this way:

"Our Father who art in heaven, Hallowed be Thy name. Thy kingdom come. Thy will be done, on earth as it is in heaven. Give us this day our daily bread. And forgive us our debts, as we also have forgiven our debtors.

"And do not lead us into temptation, but deliver us from evil."

"Listen, we've got people here that can quote stuff better than that. Why, once we got together for a fast-and-pray time. We all stuck it out for three hours, didn't eat a thing, then Bruce Bendrick ruined it.

"He went out for a drink of water, that was O.K., but came back twenty minutes later with onion on his breath! That's the last time he'll spoil one of *our* fasts! Who knows, we might have gone an hour longer if he hadn't done that."

"For if you forgive men for their transgressions, your heavenly Father will also forgive you. But if you do not forgive men, then your Father will not forgive your transgressions.

"And whenever you fast, do not put on a gloomy face as the hypocrites do; for they neglect their appearance in order to be seen fasting by men. Truly I say to you, they have their reward in full.

"But you, when you fast, anoint your head, and wash your face; so that you may not be seen fasting by men, but by your Father who is in secret; and your Father who sees in secret will repay you."

"You sure have a way with words, you know that? Listen, it's time for the bowling league tournament. First prize winner gets new bowling shoes and a leather-bound Bible. Sure can use those shoes! Want to join us? We have the best lanes of any church in town! Maybe you can win something."

"Do not lay up for yourselves treasures upon earth, where moth and rust destroy, and where thieves break in and steal; but lay up for yourselves treasures in heaven, where neither moth nor rust destroys, and where thieves do not break in or steal.

"For where your treasure is, there will your heart be also."

"Hey, now wait a minute! Where do *you* get off telling me I like material things! The good Lord said don't covet and *I* ain't about to! Course, we *all* need the bare essentials to keep going, but I DO NOT COVET!

"You wouldn't understand, dressed the way you are, but *some* of us have to spend most of our time earning money and buying things so others don't think you have to be a pauper to be a Christian! The image is important, sir, the image is important!"

"The lamp of the body is the eye; if therefore your eye is clear, your whole body will be full of light. But if your eye is bad, your whole body will be full of darkness. If therefore the light that is in you is darkness, how great is the darkness!

"No one can serve two masters; for either he will hate the one and love the other, or he will hold to one and despise the other. You cannot serve God and riches."

"You still miss the point, don't you, stranger? If you had a family to worry about you'd understand. The economy stinks! Did you know that? I've dropped a bundle on stocks and my job doesn't look too secure. Why, just last week old Harry was fired.

"How can I go to church services wearing old-style suits? My wife would be embarrassed to death! The Lord provides, but you have to be practical. Praying ain't going to fill your belly or buy you a coat."

"For this reason I say to you, do not be anxious for your life, as to what you shall eat, or what you shall drink; nor for your body, as to what you shall put on. Is not life more than food, and the body than clothing?

"Look at the birds of the air, that they do not sow, neither do they reap, nor gather into barns; and yet your heavenly Father feeds them. Are you not worth much more than they?

"And which of you by being anxious can add a single cubit to his life's span? And why are you anxious about clothing? Observe how the lilies of the field grow; they do not toil nor do they spin.

"Yet I say to you that even Solomon in all his glory did not clothe himself like one of these. But if God so arrays the grass of the field, which is alive today and tomorrow is thrown into the furnace, will He not much more do so for you, O men of little faith?

"Do not be anxious then, saying, 'What shall we eat?' or, 'What shall we drink?' or, 'With what shall we clothe ourselves?' For all these things the gentiles eagerly seek; for your heavenly Father knows that you need all these things.

"But seek first His kingdom, and His righteousness; and all these things shall be added to you."

"Well, sir, here I am wasting my time with you and I have a million errands to do."

"Therefore do not be anxious for tomorrow; for tomorrow will care for itself. Each day has enough trouble of its own."

"You know, son, if you were responsible you wouldn't be so blessed idealistic. I suggest you get a job and let the sweat pour down your face. It'd do you a world of good. And besides, you might feel more comfortable in your *own* kind of church. Pray about it . . ."

Southern Baptists and Northern Berkeley

I've been fortunate enough to experience something that causes many to shiver, shake, brag, boast or run scared. Namely—the role of guest speaker.

Perhaps a couple of real-life adventures, bubbling over with the dramatic impact of the best soap opera, would help confuse you to such a degree that never again will you have a stereotype image of either a gentile Christian or a Jewish-Christian.

First—the Southern Baptists.

These good people, although often slaves to tradition and cultural prejudices, are still among the few organized groups which tell it the way it is—God style.

I was asked to be the honored speaker at a small Southern Baptist church's banquet. The great occasion was to focus attention on abundant love flowing from the heart. I called it, as always, Valentine's Day.

My obvious topic was the heart in relation to Scripture. I prepared several quotes from both the Old and New Testaments, finding passages which I thought grabbed the soul of the Lord and what He wanted to say.

The great night arrived. I walked into a small banquet room at a local restaurant the church had rented and there was greeted by a bouncy-footed pastor and a few old gents who looked as if they were positive the South would rise again.

After writing down how many jelly beans I thought were in a large jar they seated me at the head table. About fifty persons watched this young, long-haired Jewish weirdo nervously try to bridge generation and ethnic gaps with a twitching smile.

The pastor and his wife sat to my right and my comrade-in-culture, my girl friend Anita (now my wife), sat to my left.

I figured if my suit and tie didn't convince them of my good intentions then the conservative, but very beautiful Anita would. She, too, is a Jewish-Christian and often is my key to Establishment doors.

I was pleased that no one called me "boy" or stared at me while I gracefully fingered my fried chicken during dinner.

Then the awkward introduction and fifty pair of eyes drilled me into a permanent spot behind the podium. I nodded, slapped my neatly typed three-by-five cards on the wood and proceeded.

Amazing. Utterly amazing. No one fidgeted, fussed or fumed. I simply read a passage and waited a split second for the Spirit of God to talk through me and comment on the Word.

What is this, science fiction? No, friend, it's just a promise. Who but God knows what the people need to hear? It's a matter of praying, studying and trusting.

Anyhow, I guess I spoke for a half hour, never once pulling hair from my beard, imitating a Texas accent or telling one Israeli-Arab joke.

A few seconds of silence passed after I sat down. The pastor stood, thanked me, and made several announcements having to do with church events. Wow, these dudes are something else.

Couldn't he say, "Hey, that was great, huh, team?" or "Maybe after a few years Mr. Friedman will learn something," but instead he just said "thank you" and made those announcements.

Oh, well. Pride goeth before the fall.

As the banquet broke up and the people returned to their TVs and grandchildren, several came up to me and very nicely expressed their appreciation. It was strange. I felt closer to them, because of a common faith, than I could to a Jewish friend who didn't believe in God.

All in all they were astonished that good old Jewish *chutzpah*, or nerve, could be channeled into work for the Lord. Yet, in spite of everything, the evening was *not* a complete success.

I didn't win the jelly beans.

O.K., now head north. Consider a group of persons who believe almost the same as these Southern Baptists but can't relate to anything but spiritual revolution, guerrilla Godfare and Bible bombs.

That's what I found in Berkeley. There's an international Hebrew-Christian fellowship called Beth Sar Shalom, house of the prince of peace, which has several missions in strategic bagel belts.

In San Francisco the mission is headed by a large, quiet, easy-going man by the name of Martin Rosen. Yes, some of his best relatives are Jewish.

I flew by big silver bird to the city by the bay and was picked up by Martin's secretary, a girl in her early twenties who wears a Star of David and cringes when someone calls her a gentile. She has a love for Jews that would put most rabbis to shame.

We stopped and bought the biggest variety of bagels I had ever seen: dark, light, water, egg, onion, caraway seed and on and on. Jewish soul food. Ummmmmm. That night Martin's wife mixed chopped up lox (smoked salmon) into cream cheese and I didn't care if I never moved from the table.

The bell to Martin's house rang. Again and again. All these kids (the Southerners call them "hip-eyes") filed in and sprawled on the rug, chairs and sofa. They each had a glow about their face and many carried one type of Bible or another.

Right away I knew this was no Valentine's party.

It blew my mind. So many were Jewish-Christians! One girl, Steffi Geiser, with a fantastic wit and home-grown New York flavor, told the story of how she happened to meet up with the Messiah.

The way in which God bends over backwards to reach people always stimulates my interest.

Hey—you know what it's like for Jews who are strangers to meet or come together in strange circumstances? There's a centuries-old rapport immediately established, right?

Take this feeling of an earthly tie and multiply it a thousandfold until you approach an eternal love. Man, this is what it's like every time I meet another Jewish believer.

You just kind of look at each other and, without talking, communicate with your eyes, saying, "So the Lord completed you, too! You, too, know what *He* went through only to be rejected by His own people. You, too, have tasted a never-ending love!"

It came to my turn. I perched on a stool and, this time with no notes whatsoever, I began relating my tale of how a nice, healthy, satisfied Jewish boy discovered there was more to life than death.

After I finished, another Jewish brother, recently come into the fold of spiritual Israel, told me in private how God had rescued him from one bummer after another. His words were urgent, heavy and from deep within. Rapid delivery tinged with a hesitancy resulting from too many cynical reactions from non-believers.

I nodded. Believe me, man, I *know*. But how can you explain the joy of eating a hot knish to someone who likes Spam?

Martin, with the most pleasing manner of any man I have met, had established good vibes with several communes in the San Francisco area.

Some were composed of Ph.D. drop-outs from society who clustered together in a small house somewhere in the green hills of nowhere. Others were runaway teeny boppers or frustrated youth in search of something they had once read in a fairy tale.

The one Martin took me to was a Christian commune. Several have sprung up all over California, with "baby believers" getting nursed on scriptural milk before being sent off into a world they never quite understood.

About six kids were sitting around a large living room reading the Bible. Once in a while one would smile, say "Wow, that's heavy!" or, perhaps, yawn. But it's the intentions of the heart that count . . .

It was a most unusual weekend. These brothers of mine were real Berkeleyites—real radicals and revolutionaries. They still didn't like the Establishment, but instead of trying to destroy what already has been earmarked for destruction they focused their attention on individuals seeking a fullness money can't buy.

As I boarded a plane for my trip back to Los Angeles the neat, swift, jet-set stewardess gave me a patented smile before dropping her eyes and flinching at the sight of my Bible.

So I should worry? Listen, when Elijah had his mind blown by the fiery chariot which separated him from Elisha he didn't hunt for a boarding pass. And when he was swept up by the whirlwinds he didn't hear a sweet voice asking:

"Coffee, tea or seltzer?"

Isaiah's Big Mouth

God has got this thing about letting people know He's around. It's not easy to create something as imaginative as the earth, birds, beasts and other creepies and crawlies and never receive even a cover story in *House and Gardens* for your efforts.

Yet, having all the time in the world, God has always reached those who want to be reached. In the old days (before television, radio or temple newsletters), God chose men from time to time to instruct, warn or threaten the children of Israel.

"Hold it!" you cry out again. "So what's with the prophets of Israel today? Where'd they go, huh, wise guy? And don't tell me Jeane Dixon is Jewish!"

No, man, she isn't Jewish. And she'd be in big trouble if she *did* claim to be God's prophet, since Moses said the people should stone to death anyone professing to be a prophet who errs even *once* in a prediction. And wow, has she been wrong.

It seems that God has already said a mouthful through His prophets for things concerning their time and ours, and although I believe some of God's true believers may today have the gift of prophecy for certain purposes, never again will we have a pure, 100 percent red-blooded Jewish prophet like, say, Amos's kid Isaiah.

And boy, did he talk . . .

Not only did Isaiah get all his contemporaries uptight with him, but he's been causing trouble in homes, synagogues and Zionist meetings for years and years.

Isaiah happened to hit on some very touchy subjects. Like the rebellion of Israel against God and the nature and rejection of Israel's Messiah, the Anointed One.

For example:

"Therefore the Lord Himself will give you a sign: Behold, a virgin will be with child and bear a son, and she will call His name Immanuel" (Isa. 7:14).

O.K. I've heard it all before. Yuk. Yuk. A virgin. So, "Jewish" Bibles say "young maiden" without realizing the Hebrew word used for this often meant virgin, and this fact would not be worth mentioning at all if it *didn't* since—obviously—it's not unusual for a young woman to have a child.

What about the word "Immanuel"? This can only mean "God is with us." Toss *that* around your card club. "God is with us" doesn't mean a bright rabbi said some far out things just for kicks.

Try this one on for size:

"For a child will be born to us, a son will be given to us; and the government will rest on His shoulders; and His name will be called Wonderful Counselor, Mighty God, Eternal Father, Prince of Peace" (Isa. 9:6).

You'll notice it didn't say His name was going to be called "big prophet," "good rabbi," "fair-to-middlin' carpenter" or "egomaniacal preacher." No way.

"Wonderful Counselor." Fantastic. Thousands upon thousands of the paranoid, neurotic rich or soon-to-be-bored wealthy spend untold millions every year for the privilege of stretching out on a leather couch and telling another neurotic just why they always picked lint from their navel in kindergarten.

Who understands the creation better than the Creator? And His services are accurate, loving and without a monthly bill. But you've got to *ask* for His counseling. That's the catch.

"Mighty God." Power, force and might. Yet with lightning, thunder, tidal waves, earthquakes and volcanoes, nothing is as mighty as when you can barely feel Him tapping you on the shoulder.

"Eternal Father." That's a long time. And that's the way He loves you—like a father. "Prince of Peace." There's a print making the rounds which shows a giant Jesus gently knocking on the side of the United Nations building. The Prince of Peace. He could have ended the Vietnam war in a second if both sides had appointed Him chief negotiator.

For all those who believe this Jesus is merely a figment of gentile imagination, somehow detached from Judaism, just listen to how fair God is in bestowing His eternal gifts:

"He says, 'It is too small a thing that You should be My Servant to raise up the tribes of Jacob, and to restore the preserved ones of Israel; I will also make You a light of the nations so that My salvation may reach to the end of the earth'" (Isa. 49:6).

This is not an isolated Scripture. With all the hate groups picketing and the minority groups screaming and the majority groups yelling it's difficult to arrive at a logical conclusion: God is the only One who's totally color blind.

It is for this reason that Isaiah prophesies, "Watch out, Israel, 'cause the Lord is going to lay the goodies on the gentiles as well as you." (A slight paraphrase.)

"I will also make You (the Messiah) a light of the nations (gentiles) . . ." God isn't fussy. He's not particular. He made many wonderful promises to us Jews, many of which haven't been fulfilled yet, but as far as passports to heaven are concerned He simply—is—not—partial.

We come to the "bad conscience of the synagogue," namely the 53rd chapter of Isaiah. A chapter conveniently skipped in temple readings. Why?

Read it. If you think it *describes* who you *think* it describes, don't worry. It does.

The entire book of Isaiah is really far out, but here's one last mind-blower to perhaps get you interested in this Old Testament dude who tells it like it will be:

"For all of us have become like one who is unclean, and all our righteous deeds are like a filthy garment; and all of us wither like a leaf, and our iniquities, like the wind, take us away" (Isa. 64:6).

Isaiah doesn't say, "Most of us are out of it, although a few uncles and kindhearted grandmothers are cool." Uh, uh. He says *all* have blown it. What's more, he says all of our good works (righteous deeds) are like a filthy *schmata*, or rag.

"Hold it!" you insist. "Don't tell me you aren't supposed to be nice, and good, and kind, and helpful and all those other things which the Boy Scouts teach you!"

Sure, man, why not. But can't you see the difference? On one hand *God* is able to do *His* thing through you, resulting in good works, or on the other hand *you* can say, "I'll do it myself; a holy, righteous God wouldn't punish me for being so good."

Dig it. What's good? Are you perfect? "Course not," you say, "but I can *try*." Guess what? You'll never make it.

Now don't get uptight. Just give God a break for once, O.K.? He's a perfectionist. Big deal, so that's His trip. He just happens to shudder at the thought that for eternity He'll be surrounded by imperfect creations. Rebellious creations.

Therefore He had to offer each person a chance to become perfect by accepting the Messiah, by exchanging a perfect life for an old imperfect one.

Then, in the ages to come, God can look at us, rub His eyes and say:

"*Chooooiii!* Such gentlemen I have here! Listen, each of you pick out a mansion of your choice and have fun, booby! And share the inheritance with My own Son who paid your entrance fee.

"Enjoy, enjoy!"

Saul! A Nice Jewish Boy Like You?

You've heard of St. Paul, right? He's had cathedrals, babies and popes named after him and is known as one of the heaviest apostles of this man Jesus.

Just to set the record straight, because I'm proud of this dude's fanatical loyalty to Israel and his Jewish brothers, I thought it'd be interesting to disclose the astounding fact that old Paul was actually old Saul, of Tarsus, and a devout member of the Sanhedrin.

The Sanhedrin was the group of super-religious cats, most of whom were Pharisees: being openly religious about everything they could be openly religious about.

It seems Saul had this thing against all the Jews who professed faith in the man Jesus, the One who recently had been crucified. What the Messiah's Jewish followers believed threatened Saul's position, the importance of the Sanhedrin and the number of times you could impress people by shaking ashes on your head and praying in the courtyard.

One day a man named Stephen, a Jewish believer, got the leaders so incensed at him they decided to do the only thing any civilized people would do: stone him to death.

Guess who protected their coats while they looked for sharp rocks? Right. Good old Saul. According to Scripture this Pharisee from Tarsus probably cheered "Right on!" every time a stone hit poor Stephen.

Then you know what the book of Acts says?

"And some devout men buried Stephen, and made loud lamentation over him. But Saul began ravaging the church, entering house after house; and dragging off men and women, he would put them in prison" (Acts 2:3,8).

He was a mean dude. Saul became obsessed with tormenting the Jews who were experiencing daily miracles, power and love from the same Man who just weeks before was beaten beyond recognition.

The next part really gets good. It seems Saul, "breathing threats and murder against the disciples of the Lord," got the chief's O.K. to invade the synagogues at Damascus and bring back believers, chained, to Jerusalem.

Hang on. Here goes:

"And it came about that as he journeyed, he was approaching Damascus, and suddenly a light from heaven flashed around him; and he fell to the ground, and heard a voice saying to him, 'Saul, Saul, why are you persecuting Me?'

"And he said, 'Who art Thou, Lord?' And He said, 'I am Jesus whom you are persecuting, but rise, and enter the city, and it shall be told you what you must do.'

"And the men who traveled with him stood speechless, hearing the voice, but seeing no one. And Saul got up from the ground, and though his eyes were open, he could not see; and leading him by the hand, they brought him into Damascus" (Acts 9:3-8).

Whew.

What can you say? You spend all your time hating someone, you spend all your time persecuting people because they have the audacity to believe the Messiah had come according to Scripture and was living after death, and you spend all your time on a hate campaign and then KAZAM!

Instant completion.

After a few days the Lord had faithful Ananias place his hands on Saul and the ex-Pharisee received his sight again. Then, after getting his head together after such a spiritual shock, he regained his strength on corned beef and cabbage and set off "to proclaim Jesus in the synagogues, saying 'He is the Son of God.'

"And all those hearing him continued to be amazed, and were saying, 'Is this not he who in Jerusalem destroyed those who called on this name, and who had come here for the purpose of bringing them bound before the chief priests?"

"But Saul kept increasing in strength and confounding the Jews who lived at Damascus by proving that this Jesus is the Messiah" (Acts 9:20-22).

This is equal to the Pope declaring he's going to be a rabbi, a rabbi declaring he's going to run for Pope or for the Pope and the rabbi declaring they are atheists.

Saul, bless his heart, rapped and rapped with his Jewish brothers and "proved" Jesus was the Messiah. How? Very simple. Saul, being a scholar, knew prophecies in the Scripture. As soon as the Lord removed the veil over his eyes it became obvious.

So this dude who persecuted the early saints became one of the greatest himself. And you wonder, of course, why he copped out and changed his name to Paul. Business? Easier to say?

Not quite. The Lord clued him in that he'd be preaching to the gentiles, and a Greek name would go over better. All the Scripture says is, "But Saul, who was also known as Paul . . ." Thereafter he is called Paul.

Go ahead. Read the book of Acts. I dare ya. I *double* dare ya. It tells how this Jewish big shot became humbled and trusted God for continual deliverance and power to heal the sick and cast demons out of the unfortunate.

You don't believe in demons? Phooey. So what do you think is with these guys who freak out and commit horrible crimes, who remain cool and commit obnoxious deeds, who generally remain nasty and mean and selfish and hateful and greedy and sadistic and . . .

Listen, man. Know what this rabbi Saul had to say after being hassled with everything from stoning, to ship wrecks to solitary confinement?

"For our (believers) struggle is not against flesh and blood, but against the rulers, against the powers, against the world-forces of this darkness, against the spiritual forces of wickedness in the heavenly places" (Eph. 6:12).

So next time don't be in such a hurry to criticize your parents, mother-in-law or chick for getting on you and bumming you out. Just look at them quietly and say:

"Gee, golly, and like that. You must have a demon, huh?"

Then again, for us Hebrew-Christians certain family or friends may be inclined to think *we* have demons after declaring our faith in the Lord. Their response is predictable, or, as the apostle's family said:

"Saul! A nice Jewish boy like you?"

Chicken Soup and Jesus

On a dark night, when the old lady was sacked out and the crowds had returned home, Rabbi Nicodemus snuck out of his pad and came to visit this Yeshua, or Joshua, or Jesus.

Big Nick knew something was different about this Man and decided *He* must be a great prophet of God. The Messiah, in answer to Nick's inquiries, said in order to enter the Kingdom of God you must be born again.

"Hah!" Nick replied, "you think I'm a dummy? How can an old man crawl back into his mother's womb and be born again?"

Jesus just folded His arms, smiled patiently and

said Nick would have to be born of the *Spirit*, not just the flesh.

Ah! Spiritual rebirth! So *that's* the key!

When you accept Messiah as your Saviour, the One who was the final Passover lamb, the One who paid our debts—then you are born spiritually, you have the gift of God within you. Even a Reform temple's prayer book reads:

"God of Abraham, Isaac and Jacob . . . thank you for implanting eternal life within us."

O.K. Let's say you accept Him. You've got His Spirit within you. What else do you have? Heart burn? Acid indigestion? Naw, something worse. Your *old* self.

Decision time. You can tune in to *Him* or you can tune in to *you*. Dig? That's why so-called "Christians" you meet are often exactly the same as anyone else. They haven't tuned in to Him.

But at least they have the choice.

Hey, remember way back in Genesis when God promised those goodies to Abraham? Unconditionally? Well—hang on to your *yarmulke* 'cause God means what he says.

The Bible assures us one day the land will be ours, the great majestic kingdom which many Orthodox Jews are waiting for today will come, and the only price of admission will be the same as it was for Daddy Abraham.

Believe.

The most imaginative Utopia ever created by a writer will not compare to the beautiful world which the King of kings will usher in. Clean air. Fresh water. Jewish soul food. And best of all, an eternal brilliance, the glory of God, lighting our world. Yep, chicken soup and Jesus.

Question: Do you have to wait until you die to find out if you've been on a bad trip or not?

Answer: No way.

You can find out now, today, by searching the Scriptures, by searching for God. In Jeremiah 29:13 God says:

"And you will seek Me and find Me, when you search for Me with all your heart."

Hey, listen. All these science freaks are claiming we're on a collision course with ourselves, right? The world can't go on before we all wipe each other out with bombs, starve to death or pollute ourselves to oblivion.

Former activists who were looking for greedy, selfish, ambitious men to save greedy, selfish ambitious men have discovered something: man is too greedy, selfish and ambitious to pull it off.

A bad case of the empties.

The spiritual empties. So I invite you to go to your local Spirit service station and fill up. It might be your chair, standing in the shower, eating breakfast, walking the dog or praying at midnight in the parking lot of a church.

Get rid of the empties and fill up with Messiah. It's a permanent job. Complete. Final. You'll never run dry again. It works on both Jewish and gentile models—any year, any make.

And don't worry about your windshield. It'll be spotless. But instead of just wiping the outside, this eternal love of God will present you with an inside job, down to the heart, where it counts.

"Surely I am more stupid than any man,
  And I do not have the understanding
     of a man.
  And I have not learned wisdom,
  But I have knowledge of the Holy One.
  Who has ascended into heaven
     and descended?
  Who has gathered the wind
     in His fists?
  Who has wrapped the waters
     in His garment?
  Who has established all the ends
     of the earth?
  What is His name or His son's name?
  Surely you know!"

Proverbs 30

Into the Spirit

About six months after I had stepped into the strange new world of a Jewish believer in Messiah I stepped into an even stranger world of the supernatural.

I was alone in my bachelor apartment, furnished with a donated couch and swaying bed, when a wave of depression hit me from almost out of nowhere. I couldn't explain it. I couldn't pinpoint it. Yet the weight on my shoulders and swirling dark cloud around my head *had* to mean something.

Gritting my teeth, I begrudgingly thought to myself: *I'm a Jewish believer in Messiah Jesus now. Guess I should pray.* Sitting at my kitchen table, I opened my mouth, intending to start off with something brilliant like "Dear Lord . . ."

Nothing came out. Zilch. I tried again. Not a sound. The "dear Lord" echoing in my head refused to vocalize itself. *What's going on here?* I tried it again. Nothing. Then, before I had a chance to dial a friend and, quite obviously, say nothing over the phone, an awesome, eerie, scintillating *something* happened.

Words began to fly from my mouth with reckless abandon. It wasn't Spanish—I had taken that in high school. It wasn't French—I had taken *that* in college. What was it? I didn't know—and I didn't care.

For thirty minutes I felt as if I was floating from here to there to everywhere. The depression was replaced by euphoria. I sensed the presence of the Lord whom I had so recently met. I became calm, peaceful, confused . . .

Then it hit me. Aha! This has to be what lay persons speaking churchese call "tongues," or glossolalia. HOLD IT! DON'T MOVE! Give me a chance and I'll put the whole thing in perspective for you, because, after all, Messiah Jesus *is* the same yesterday, today and tomorrow.

Don't throw the baby out with the bath water, and all that, old chap . . .

I began a study of Scripture which proved to me that this phoenomena was definitely for today (although abused or counterfeited by individuals or groups). On the other end of the spiritual spectrum are the head-trippers, the Bible intellectuals who conclude the Holy Spirit went on vacation just as the Apostle John bit the dust.

My church had never discussed "gifts of the spirit" or how they are to be used in the corporate body of believers. I had never heard anything against *or* for present-day use of prophecy, word of knowledge, discerning of spirits, healing, administration, etc.

I did notice that every pastor, regardless of his beliefs on this subject, *did* believe in the gifts of pastor-teacher. After all, that's who they were!

Without belaboring this point, "spirit-filled" believers who treat "unspirit-filled" believers as second-class Christians are grieving the very Spirit they wear on their sleeve. *Every* believer is Spirit-indwelled, that's what separates us from non-believers.

If a certain believer has not yet opened himself up to the *fullness* of the Spirit then patience is required, not ridicule.

At the other extreme, those who study the Word, as well they should, but who put down all "gifts of the Spirit" as being a thing of the past, are grieving the very Spirit Who breathed life into the Word.

Meanwhile, did I tell you about that weird Bible study I went to? No? O.K., here it is.

My good friends Paul and Leonore Herne have a Bible study each week at their Beverly Hills home. My wife Anita and I had already spent two years in Dallas, experiencing the glare from the buckle on the Bible belt.

Now, about four years after my apartment experience, we found ourselves at the Hernes, speaking with several Jewish believers after an excellent message by Bob Weiner, another member of the tribe.

"Anyone who wants to be prayed for healing, join Bob Weiner in the other room," Leonore announced.

Anita followed Bob and the others. I opted for the punch and strudel.

On the way home that evening my dear wife explained how she had seen legs grow in length on two different women during the prayer time.

"Hey, I should have been there," I laughed.

"Why's that?" Anita replied.

"Because one of my legs is shorter than the other."

"God's everywhere, isn't he? She almost jumped at the opportunity. What could I do? Argue? We arrived home, I sat on the couch, Anita grabbed my ankles and prayed. *Click. Click. Click.* My short leg was no longer short.

"Fantastic! Praise God! Now let's go for another six inches!" I screamed. After all, when you're only five feet four you've gotta grab at anything you can. Needless to say, we were thankful for the half-inch I received. I'll wait for the six . . .

Soon after this, following a Bible study at our own home, I related what had happened to a close friend. His wife beamed with excitement and informed me one of her husband's arms was at least an inch shorter than the other, and she always had to shorten one sleeve on each of his shirts.

Ignorance is bliss. I acted—not knowing one scripture on healing, *why* we have the authority to pray as we do, etc.

"Hey, here's how it works!" I pushed my friend against the kitchen wall, making sure his shoulders were pressed back. "Now extend your arms!" He did. Sure enough, one arm was at least an inch shorter than the other. I grabbed his wrists and bowed my head.

108

"Heavenly Father," I began, "thank you for healing this arm. For lengthening it. In Jesus name we . . ." The words had scarcely left my lips before I heard the faintest *click, click, click*. I opened my eyes in time to see the short arm grow out to equal the other.

"Praise God!" This came from his wife, not from the healee. The healer, Messiah Jesus, must have been amused to observe my friend staring blankly into space. I thought he was overcome with joy, speechless in the face of this miracle.

"I don't believe it," he whispered.

"What?!! Look!!"

"It didn't happen."

"Of course it did! Look! Why didn't it happen?!"

"Because my home church in Indiana never taught you could be healed."

"But you just *were* healed! Your arm *has* grown! Look! Who cares about your little church in Indiana?!" I was exasperated, to say the least.

My friend sighed deeply and once more: "Gee, I don't know, they didn't teach it." Right after this his wife lengthened one sleeve on each shirt. So he'd look good. On his next trip to Indiana.

It was Derby Day, 1977, before I discovered the Lord could heal more than once in a lifetime. Why Derby Day? Because our friends, Ray and Marian Sandbek, were from Louisville where the annual running of the horses was more important than a free wing at Colonel Sanders'.

To wit: a Derby Day party with mostly church friends attending. No gambling mind you. Just a nice fellowship with a two minute break to watch a bunch of four-legged brown blurs see which one could wind up where it started from the fastest.

Just like a lot of people we know . . .

Anyway, the Sandbek's were moving back to Louisville and Anita felt very bad that Ray was ready to leave—bad knee and all. He had had surgery, with the kneecap replaced with a synthetic substitute.

"Let's pray for him," she asked/ordered.

"Sure."

Ray was game. We went into a bedroom, layed hands on his knee and thanked the Lord that He still heals, that with the stripes of Messiah we *are* healed (Isaiah 53) and that that knee better shape up and conform to the Word of God!

The heat from the Spirit was intense, pouring through Anita's and my hands, right into that old knee. After about a minute Ray fully extended his leg.

"Hmmm, couldn't do that before," he mumbled. Then he pulled his leg up, his calf tight against his thigh. "Hmmm, couldn't do that before."

"Is it healed, Ray?" we asked.

"Yep."

We didn't call Ray "Mr. Excitement" for nothing. He was very cool, very unemotional, very thankful. For the first time he snuck up on his sweet wife Marian without hearing the tell tale *click-click* of his knee which always preceded his arrival.

Anita was going for the whole shootin' match. She felt the Spirit was so heavy that whoever wanted to be healed at that time would be. We walked out into the living room and ran into John Lockwood, in a great deal of pain.

John had begun to play professional football for the Los Angeles Rams before being injured. Rather than risk being a crippled NFL veteran he went into coaching high school football.

On this same day he was holding his left hand belt high, unable to raise it any higher because of a severe rip between his major and minor pectoral muscles. The inside of his huge left bicep was filled with hemorrhaging blood. The injury was a result of a wrestling match with one of his students.

We quickly explained how the Lord has just healed Ray, and . . . what does he have to lose? Nothing of course, so he followed us into the room. We layed hands on them ol' muscles, believing Messiah is the great healer (Ex. 15:26).

Once again, the heat was intense. Once again, a healing took place. John smiled—a much bolder reaction than Ray had given us. Within ten minutes John was lifting his arm head high, explaining he felt as if the lower pectoral muscle was being lifted up and "knitted together" to the higher one.

Within thirty minutes John could move his arm anyway he wished. He even flexed his chest muscles up and down to prove they had been healed.

Showoff.

John's healing was not an end unto itself. Being naturally shy, John didn't have much opportunity to share his faith in the Lord with his students that often. But after his miraculous healing *they* insisted on knowing why he didn't require several weeks of therapy to be healed as the doctors had predicted.

John told 'em!

Now John, his beautiful wife Lynda and their children live near Boulder, Colo. where the ex-football coach is a proprietor of an antique shop. I'm sure he can lift the heavy pieces all by himself . . .

If you're wondering what all of this has to do with being Jewish and believing in Messiah Jesus it has *everything* to do with it. After all, *our* prophets were the ones who healed the sick and brought the dead back to life! (2 Kings 5, I Kings 17)

By the close of this remarkable day we were faced with a decision: turn our back on God and check His healing power, which we couldn't do, or somehow introduce this possibly "foreign" idea into our church's Sunday School.

We opted for the latter. I think I'd rather have been an Old Testament prophet, thousands of years ago, far away from church . . .

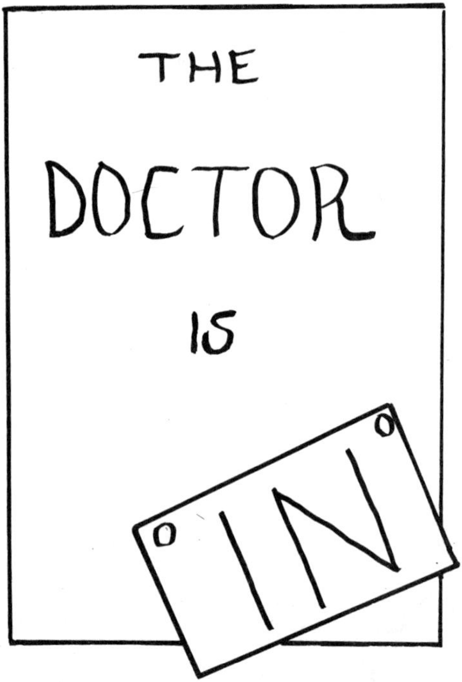
THE
DOCTOR
IS
IN

Jesus of Nazareth, M.D.
a public corporation

Several of those attending the Derby Day party were members of the Mariners Sunday School class of the First Presbyterian Church of Hollywood, where I have been a member for several years.

WHAT?!! What happened to the Baptist?!! The closest thing I can figure is that we lost him on the freeway. At a swap meet? Garage sale? What can I say? Denominations are neither here nor there with me. What counts is the individual place of worship, that the Bible is taught as the inerrant Word of God and the Holy Spirit isn't asked to take a seat in the back pew.

Yes, it's true. I found myself as both teacher and

president of the Mariners (and we never went sailing once). When the time came to introduce the concept of Jesus as healer to the class there were as many opinions as people.

Very boldly, mind you, I suggested that anyone wishing to be prayed for—for physical, emotional or spiritual healing—please meet us behind a partition on the dark side of the room.

How's that for throwing light onto a subject?

Eventually we changed rooms and held our "time of prayer and healing" atop a little stage in our new meeting place. I really wasn't the prime instigator and boat-rocker as far as stepping into the Spirit was concerned. Others had preceded me.

Two years prior to my term of office Walt and Glenellen Maxwell were presidents. Glennie really knows how to cut through the games and garbage and sweetly, *very* sweetly, focus everyone's attention on Jesus.

Then along came Siegfried and Inge Cesh. Sieggy is my very own brother in the Lord, closer than a physical brother ever could be. He once melted an iceberg by smiling at it. And, at any given moment, Sieggy can place his arm around a hurting soul and make roses grow where, moments before, only tumbleweeds were.

When Sieggy speaks it's as if a sword of truth pierces you to your spirit and soul BUT—immediately the healing oil of gladness soothes the wound and makes you better than new.

There I was—following Sieggy and not only encouraging our class to pray for our brothers and sisters behind the Iron Curtain, as Sieggy had done, but to also reach out their hands and receive all Messiah Jesus has for them.

It took quite a while for others from the church to shyly approach our group and ask for prayer, but those who did often received healing beyond their wildest imagination.

It is not my intention to present a theological examination of divine healing, and why it is so powerfully in operation today as it ever was. I did write a thorough pamphlet on the subject which we offer to all who come for prayer.

Joining us in praying for others was Karen Huffman, who never limits the Lord in anything. She wanted to share what we had discovered with her sister and brother-in-law, Juanita and Joe Dunlap of Wichita, Kansas.

Off we flew to the flatlands. During an informal time of sharing the good news at the Dunlaps I noticed Joe was intentionally fading into the wall. He's a police officer, and had just injured the achilles' tendon on one foot.

He finally consented to let us pray for him and—you guessed it—he was back at work within a couple of days rather than several weeks! Not only did Joe become a preachin' cop, but Juanita got so turned on she never found the off switch! She's now a much sought after speaker in her home town!

Once you grab a little of the Lord's goodies it's easy to become hooked. We wanted more—and found more.

Our class had a number of Jewish believers attending, including Richard and Eva Pepper. Richard has survived as a junior high school teacher (now *that's* a miracle) and Eva's time is taken up with the likes of Aaron, Brenna and Ethan (such *nachas*!). All the children must sing "I'm a Pepper, you're a Pepper . . ."

We'd have a group of about eight meeting once a week at the Peppers. To pray, to share, to wait on the Lord, to bless the Lord, to see just *what* the Lord would do. *Baruch ha shem*, he did a lot!

Often someone would pray "In the Spirit," or in "tongues" and another would interpret. A message of encouragement, of power, of hope. We would pray for one another's needs and see prayer answered: sometimes immediately, sometimes far down the road, sometimes in ways we hadn't thought about.

A "word of knowledge" might spring up, with the Lord revealing information to one about another which would help in the person's coping with a present situation or preparing for the future.

Maybe a tuned-in fellow such as Stan Kojack would speak words of prophecy, thereby encouraging, even urging those present to be real *menches.* and my dear wife Anita would pray on behalf of others, often crying as she felt their hurt, or laughing as she felt their joy.

Another time Daisy Vollrath, one of the most loving young ladies I've ever met, came for prayer before traveling to East Germany for a visit with "imprisoned" believers.

As we prayed I had a vision of a room, and described it to Daisy, as well as the people in the room and what they were wearing. One woman in particular seemed troubled and I informed Daisy of this.

While in East Germany Daisy met with a group of

believers, recognized the room I had described—and the woman—and was able to counsel and console her the rest of the day.

My friend, God is not asleep or buried in "philosophy of religion" textbooks. He's alive—and well—and active! If the Spirit of the Lord is not moving in your life it's because *you've* shut Him out. He *enjoys* blessing His children.

Small group interaction is critical for the Spirit to act as Himself and bring awe, wonders, signs and words among those who have believed in the name of Messiah Jesus.

And the *gifts* of the Spirit, so wonderfully bestowed, should only be a happy result of coming together to praise and worship our Lord. In fact, the tribe of Judah ("Praise") led the nation of Israel into battle.

If you lead with praise your battles will turn into passing annoyances, and your annoyances into distant memories.

Meanwhile, back at Hollywood Pres . . .

Our "Time of Prayer and Healing" moved into a small chapel following the second service, with Pastor Ralph Osborne leading our group. I joined other elders as well as mere "laymen" (same Spirit, same gifts, no title . . .) in praying for sweet souls.

Our senior pastor, John Lloyd Ogilvie, is an anointed man of God whose blue eyes have such depth and intensity, such love and wisdom, it seems possible to go on a "spiritual high" just by looking at them.

Other congregations are springing up all over the country, many attempting to bridge the cultural gap often existing between Jewish and gentile believers.

Louis Lapides is pastor of Beth Ariel Fellowship, meeting in Brentwood, on the west side of Los Angeles. A Jewish believer, Pastor Lapides clings to the New Covenant Scripture declaring that the Messiah has "broken down the barrier of the dividing wall" between Jew and gentile, that as a "kingdom of priests," Israel was to turn the world to the one Lord God, and now—as both Jewish and gentile believers—we are, together, to turn all who would receive Him to the same God.

We are to pray together—worship together—enjoy each other's company—study His Word—and be as one body with Messiah Jesus as the head.

Israel was "chosen" to proclaim the name of the Lord among the goyim, not to become an isolated sect in the hills of Judea and Samaria, the Galilee and the Negev, keeping all others away. The Lord gave us the land of Israel to enjoy, to live on, to prosper and multiply on.

The Messiah came first to Israel, then the world, to love, and to be loved by, all.

Yet often we wonder if love is enough to get us through the day, to face the week, to prepare for next month. The world seems to be falling apart with everyone complaining about it and no one doing anything about it.

Each week on "Friedman & Friends,"a program I produce, write and host for Trinity Broadcasting Network, we discuss not only the Jewishness of the Scriptures and of Messiah Jesus, but also what affect this information might have on your personal life.

Why do so many see psychiatrists for ten or twenty years, often pinpointing the "problems" but never coming up with any solutions? Why do so many get into—then out of—various "isms" and "ologies"?

Why do so many try *anything* but Messiah Jesus?

You either believe in God or you don't. For those of you who believe in God, you may or may not believe in the personality of a devil, or satan, or the fallen Lucifer. Isaiah did (chapter 14). Ezekiel did (chapter 28).

But then again they were only prophets of the God of Israel. You're much more sophisticated than that.

Our son Michael Philip Friedman, who at this writing is eight years old, is your all-American boy. A Dodger baseball fanatic, computer enthusiast, amateur farmer, etc.

Yet once in a while when the lights are turned off in his room at night the spirits turn on. He has seen demonic apparitions trying to scare him, frighten him, confuse him.

And—praise God—he has had wonderful visions of heaven, of his grandfather who is now with the Lord—of the Messiah Himself. When the enemy is after him he has learned to take up the authority even an eight-year-old has in the Lord and to yell out: "In Jesus' name get out of here!"

Some things you have to learn to do for yourself . . .

Or, sometimes in the morning, he will matter of factly relate a most wonderful insight, vision or dream he has received. The spiritual world is as real as a Dodger double play!

Michael is as Jewish a young man as you can be. A descendant of Abraham, Isaac and Jacob. A believer in Messiah Jesus. Not a "super saint" or "goody-

goody," but rather a well-balanced man who realizes things not seen are as real as those which are.

The most absurd thing any one can say about us Jewish believers is that we're not Jewish! The most absurd thing any one can do is to reject the Jewish Messiah because they've been taught He's the Lord of the goyim!

If everything this world has to offer isn't enough for you then open up and consider what we've been saying. In this world material possessions will be gobbled up quicker than you can say "Dow Jones."

You may wake up in the morning standing naked in a vacant lot with no friends around. Then what?

There's very little time left before the Messiah returns to reign in Jerusalem over all the earth. Now's the time to build a foundation for yourself, so when the storms hit your feet will stand firm.

The best foundation is rock. Messiah Jesus *is* the rock. Moses knew that. The prophets knew that. All looked forward to the time of Messiah.

Now is the time to receive Him, to be filled with His Spirit, to become all the Lord God desires you to become: a unique, intelligent, gifted vessel containing the very Spirit of God Himself, flowing in love and power, bringing peace to all you meet.

Let's pray:

"Heavenly Father, God of Abraham, Isaac and Jacob, thank you for loving me and accepting me just as I am. I can confess I have sinned, or rebelled against you, but now I turn from the past and toward you. Thank you for Messiah Jesus taking our iniquities upon Himself while hanging on the tree, then offering to me new, everlasting life as He rose from the dead.

"Messiah Jesus—come into my heart and fill me with your Holy Spirit. Empower me to live in you, as you abide in me. Thank you, Father, for my salvation, in Messiah Jesus' name I pray. Amen."